The National
BASEBALL HALL OF FAME
Collection

The National
BASEBALL HALL OF FAME
Collection

CELEBRATING THE GAME'S GREATEST PLAYERS

by JAMES BUCKLEY JR.

EPIC INK

Brimming with creative inspiration, how-to projects, and useful information to enrich your everyday life, Quarto Knows is a favorite destination for those pursuing their interests and passions. Visit our site and dig deeper with our books into your area of interest: Quarto Creates, Quarto Cooks, Quarto Homes, Quarto Lives, Quarto Drives, Quarto Explores, Quarto Gifts, or Quarto Kids.

© 2020 National Baseball Hall of Fame
Text © 2020 James Buckley Jr.

Published in 2020 by Epic Ink, an imprint of The Quarto Group,
11120 NE 33rd Place, Suite 201, Bellevue, WA 98004 USA.
www.QuartoKnows.com

Epic Ink titles are also available at discount for retail, wholesale, promotional, and bulk purchase. For details, contact the Special Sales Manager by email at specialsales@quarto.com or by mail at The Quarto Group, Attn: Special Sales Manager, 100 Cummings Center Suite 265D, Beverly, MA 01915 USA.

20 21 22 23 24   5 4 3 2 1

ISBN: 978-0-7603-6934-0

Digital edition published in 2020
eISBN: 978-0-7603-7018-6

Library of Congress Cataloging-in-Publication Data available upon request.

Printed, manufactured, and assembled in Shenzhen, China, 06/20

MIX
Paper from
responsible sources
FSC® C017606

#338815

CONTENTS

★ ★ ★ ★ ★ ★

FOREWORD

★ ★ ★

WHEN THE GAME ON THE NIGHT OF SEPT. 6, 1995, became official, I was not thinking about history.

It was a beautiful night in Baltimore and we just took the lead against the California Angels, who were in the thick of the pennant race. In the bottom of the fourth, Bobby Bonilla led off the inning with a home run and I followed closely behind with a home run to left field. I was never considered a fast guy but I felt like I flew around the bases after that!

When fellow Hall of Famer Mike Mussina retired the Angels in order in the top of the fifth, the fans at Camden Yards started cheering and simply wouldn't stop. Twenty-two minutes straight. It was amazing. On the wall of the B&O Warehouse what had become a nightly ritual of the numbers dropping to lead up to this night, the "2,130" changed to "2,131."

It was a celebration of the game – more about baseball and less about me. I never set out to break Lou Gehrig's record. The streak that started on May 30, 1982 was born out of a simple principle taught to me by my dad. As a ballplayer, your job is to show up each and every day ready to play. And if the manager believes you are one of the nine guys who gives the team the best chance to win that day, he will play you.

But more than 13 years later, The Streak had come to mean many things to many people. I loved hearing stories about other people's streaks, be it school or work or volunteering—truly inspiring people who, well, just showed up and were there for their teammates.

My teammates Bobby Bonilla and Rafael Palmeiro told me that the only way to get the game restarted was if I took a lap around the park. I told them they were crazy, and they essentially shoved me down the first base line. As I slowly made my way down the right field line, I started to shake hands and see familiar faces, and the celebration went from 46,272 people to very much one-on-one.

As I circled the park, the appreciation of the fans washed over me. Our national pastime had endured a difficult work stoppage the year before, but this night showed that the love of the game was stronger than any of our challenges. These fans were waiting for a chance to celebrate baseball.

I look back today and see the helmet I wore that night, now on exhibit at the National Baseball Hall of Fame and Museum. It serves as a connection to that moment 25 years ago, something that brings us all back to Camden Yards.

Baseball's history is full of such moments, and we all have memories of the game that stay with us forever.

As I walk through the Hall of Fame on my visits to Cooperstown, it is an honor to see my artifacts on display. This amazing place tells the story of the game's rich history, which is woven into the fabric of our country. No place I know expressed that better than the National Baseball Hall of Fame.

As you enjoy this look at the Hall of Fame's collection, I hope you relive and remember the events that shaped your love of the game. It is our shared history that turns baseball into an unbreakable bond for fans and families across the country and around the world.

— CAL RIPKEN JR.
MARCH 2020

Cal Ripken Jr.: Baltimore Orioles SS/3B (1981–2001), 1982 AL Rookie of the Year, two-time AL MVP (1983 and 1991), 19-time All-Star, 9-time Silver Slugger winner, 1992 Roberto Clemente Award winner, and elected a member of the National Baseball Hall of Fame in 2007.

INTRODUCTION

★ ★ ★

BASEBALL HAS A DEEP AND ABIDING HISTORY, a permanent, ongoing connection to not just its own past, but to the history of America itself. The game was forged on grass about the same time our Union was forged in war. It grew from pastoral settings to urban playgrounds as farms gave way to cities and suburbs. Baseball as commerce expanded with the growing commercial world of modern America. At every point in the past century, the game has intersected with the wider society. And in recent years, though it's been international since its earliest days, baseball has had a greater connection with the wider world of sport as well.

No one knows who threw the first pitch in baseball, but most historians point to the 1850s and 1860s as the period when various ball games coalesced into a game recognizable to today's bleacher creatures. Leap forward to 1936 when the National Baseball Hall of Fame Museum was born as its first class was elected. Three years later, the famous brick building in Cooperstown, a lovely village in upstate New York's Catskill region, opened and gave baseball's immortals a permanent home.

And who would earn a place in that home? Who would take up residence in this new Mt. Olympus of baseball? And who would decide?

Then, as now, the members of the Hall of Fame are nearly all chosen by the Baseball Writers' Association of America. The writers who have earned a voting place in that body by dint of long service choose from among a slate of players who have been out of baseball for at least five years and played at least ten. By an up-or-down vote on their ballots, the writers decide if they think the player has the qualities needed to earn a place in Cooperstown. A "yes" vote of 75 percent or higher means that player will be given a place in baseball history.

But, from among the dozens of players to choose from as each balloting season rolls around, what makes a person truly a Hall of Famer? What qualities place them above the everyday professional and move them into the stratosphere of their chosen profession, set them above and apart from the good and the merely great? In the stories in this book, we'll try to briefly show those qualities for the players, umpires, managers, and executives featured. Baseball fans obsess about statistics, and stats rightly play an enormous role in determining membership in this exclusive club. But as recent Hall of Fame elections have shown, entry into Cooperstown's Plaque Gallery comes from more than numbers, wins and losses, homers, and hits. It takes something special, something unique, to make it in baseball and into the Hall of Fame.

For some players, it's an ability to overcome something on or off the field to succeed. For others, it is an inner strength that lets them go beyond their particular skills and use their mental toughness to augment their physical talent. No matter how blessed a person is with that physical ability, it is the rare marriage of talent, determination, hard work, and luck that carves a path through baseball history and ends in a little village in upstate New York.

SPECIAL FEATURES

This book is packed with photos of the Hall of Fame's treasures, those pieces of gear, paperwork, and artifacts that give reality to what are, for today's fans, memories of baseball's greatest players and moments. Seeing these objects brings those people and their deeds back to life, if only in the mind's eye.

VISITING COOPERSTOWN

★ At least once in every baseball fan's life, he or she should travel up New York's Route 80, past farms and barns and little towns, over hill and dale and diner . . . to Cooperstown. Whether the place was actually a part of baseball's birth or not (it wasn't), it doesn't really matter anymore. For nearly 80 years, Cooperstown has been more than a bucolic destination for vacationers seeking baseball and a lakeside idyll. It has overcome the fact of history and become the dream destination for anyone who loves the game.

The classic brick building has undergone several extensive renovations, with the result being that the Hall of Fame today is an impressive, entertaining, and beautiful museum of baseball. Room after room catalogs the heroes, the moments, the pioneers, the champions. Visitors see the spikes Hank Aaron wore, the uniform Lou Gehrig made famous, the bat Roberto Clemente wielded, and the cap that Christy Mathewson put on to take the mound. From the game's earliest twinklings to the bright stars of today's heroes, all are featured in the Hall's numerous displays, films, and exhibitions. And yes, the Museum Shop is awesome.

Visit www.baseballhall.org to find out more, including tips on traveling the road that lies across the green hills like the unraveled stitching of a baseball.

1

THE PITCHERS

Every pitch is an anticipation. As the pitcher stands on the mound, peering in for the sign, he is potential energy. He has frozen time, in a way. Nothing will happen until he makes it happen. He's in control. He has the attention of everyone around him. His upcoming pitch will be for good or ill, and at that tiny moment of inaction, no one knows what will come next. Not even him. Of course, he then has to leave that island of perfection, that moment of nothing-bad/nothing-good, and become kinetic energy.

He flows into motion, the ball leaves his hand . . . and it begins. There is action, reaction, ball or strike, hit or miss, fair or foul. A result. And then, the frozen moment returns . . . and the game goes on.

Pitching is a combination of physical skill, mental energy, and not a little bit of artistry. Power helps, sure, but simple speed is not enough. It takes craft, brains, timing, guts. To move beyond "just get it over" and into the realm of "unhittable" takes a special athlete, a special person. This chapter covers many of those special men, pitchers who thawed those frozen moments successfully enough to succeed wonderfully. More than 7,500 players have thrown a pitch in the Major Leagues; 83 of them earned a place in the Hall of Fame as pitchers.

OPPOSITE: **Dizzy Dean**

GROVER ALEXANDER

A member of the third class inducted into the Hall of Fame, Alexander's legacy stems from a career of greatness—and an afternoon of bravery. He started strong by winning 28 games as a rookie in 1911, and from 1915 to 1917 he won the pitching Triple Crown each season. His 33 wins in 1916 have not been matched since, and his 1.22 ERA in 1915 has been topped only once. However, a year in France in World War I left him shell-shocked. His epilepsy was more prevalent when he returned as well. However, he persevered and played until 1929. That afternoon of bravery? Game Seven of the 1926 World Series. Pitching for the Cardinals after a complete-game win in Game Six, Alexander struggled to the mound to face powerful Tony Lazzeri with the bases loaded. The pitcher they called "Pete" struck out Lazzeri and went on to win the game and the Series for St. Louis. Alexander didn't earn his place in the Hall for that one moment, but he did earn a place in the history of guts.

TOP: *Grover Alexander*
RIGHT: *Jack Chesbro*
OPPOSITE: *Mordecai "Three-Finger" Brown*
captured doing what he did best.

MORDECAI BROWN

Most fans know this hurler more for his famous nickname, "Three-Finger," than for his prodigious pitching performances. Why Three-Finger? A farm accident when he was only seven years old left him with a stub of an index finger and two other badly bent fingers. But to focus on this is to miss out on the bigger story: Consider that in a dead-ball era dominated by great pitchers, Brown stood out as one of the best, and helped the Cubs win two World Series. Turns out his disability informed his pitching abilities, giving him movement on the ball unlike any other.

JACK CHESBRO

Hundreds of pitchers have put together great seasons since 1904, but none have matched Jack Chesbro's 41-win mark that season. The spitballer not only won, he finished what he started for the New York Highlanders (as the Yankees were known then). He threw 48 complete games that season, more than today's pitchers could do in two careers.

NICKNAMES GALORE

Rube. Lefty. Cy. The Big Train. Big Six. Pud. Old Hoss. And that's just from the list of Hall of Fame pitchers, most from before World War II. And how could we forget the Wild Hoss of the Osage, Schnozz, and of course Bob "Death to Flying Things" Ferguson? Or "The Only" Nolan? From baseball's earliest days, fans and the media have long loved to create colorful shorthand for their favorite players. Each era has spawned its own list of marvelous monikers. Stan "The Man" and the Splendid Splinter were World War II-era favorites. The Say-Hey Kid and the Mick roamed the outfield in the 1950s and 1960s. Mr. October made the 1970s jump. In the 1990s, The Big Unit (below) steamed along much as the Big Train had. In recent seasons fans have cheered for Big Papi, the Big Hurt, and the Big Maple, to say nothing of A-Rod, Joey Bats, Krush, and, of course, Thor. Need to know the players' real names? As your grand-dad has said since he watched a certain Babe . . . Look 'em up!

JAMES GALVIN

The man they called "Pud" played a game with which modern fans and pitchers are simply not familiar. He pitched often, he completed games, and he won . . . over and over. In a career spent entirely in the 19th century, he set remarkably high standards; to this day he holds three career records: most complete games, losses, and hits in one league. His endurance was his most impressive asset: In 1883 he started 75 games . . . and finished 72. And he won 46 of them.

WALTER JOHNSON

Baseball as a going concern was more than fifty years old when the first class of the Hall of Fame was chosen in 1936. Of the first five men chosen for the Hall, only two were pitchers. One was Walter Johnson, "The Big Train." Long-limbed, unflappable, and nearly impossible to hit or faze, Johnson was fated to be the great pitcher on a series of bad teams. How bad? Of the 279 games he lost, his Senators teammates didn't score in nearly a quarter. Still, his numbers are stunning: 110 shutouts, an all-time best; 3,512 strikeouts, the most until Steve Carlton (and later, others) topped him in 1983; 417 wins, second behind Cy Young; a 2.36 career ERA.

OLD JUDGE CIGARETTES Goodwin & Co., New York.

OLD JUDGE CIGARETTES Goodwin & Co., New York.

ABOVE: *James Galvin, Tim Keefe*

LEFT: *Walter Johnson perfected a whipping, sidearm motion that gave great movement to an already tough-to-hit fastball.*

ADDIE JOSS

In baseball's "what might have been" category, one must certainly put this amazing yet ill-fated young player. He began his career in 1902 with a one-hitter (and that one hit a disputed one) and powered through a series of ever-more-impressive seasons, including twice posting AL-best ERAs amid a six-year ML-best string in which his highest ERA was 2.01. His finest moment—and one of the finest in baseball history—came in a crucial late-season game in 1908. Facing Ed Walsh, himself a future fellow Hall member, Joss needed to win for his Naps team. While Walsh nearly bottled up Cleveland, Joss was literally perfect. Among baseball's 23 perfect games through 2019, only Don Larsen's World Series gem in 1956 meant more to his team's success than Joss's. Sadly, three years later, he was dead at 31 of meningitis. Given that he still has an impressive career ERA of 1.89 and the lowest base runners per nine innings mark ever (8.73), one can only wonder what he might have accomplished with the gift of more time.

TIM KEEFE

A 19th-century star, Keefe had his greatest success with the Giants. His stunning 1888 campaign included 35 wins (featuring 19 in a row) and an NL-best 1.74 ERA. And here's one you won't see again: in an 1884 Championship Series between Charles Radbourn's Grays and Keefe's Mets, Keefe pitched the first two games . . . and then umpired the third!

ABOVE: *After the much-loved Addie Joss died at 31 of meningitis, an all-star baseball game was held to raise money for his family.*

TEAMS OF LONG AGO

★ Not every team has been able to withstand the long-term rigors of life as a Major League club. In the early days of the NL (before 1901) and in the old American Association (1882–1891), teams came and went with surprising speed. Yet some managed to attract occasional Hall of Fame talent. Here's a sampling of now-defunct teams and some of the Hall members who wore their fleeting colors.

TEAM	YEARS	HALL OF FAME PLAYERS
BUFFALO BISONS	1879–1885	Dan Brouthers, Pud Galvin, Jim O'Rourke
CLEVELAND SPIDERS	1887–1899	Jesse Burkett, John Clarkson, George Davis, Buck Ewing, Bobby Wallace, Cy Young
LOUISVILLE COLONELS	1882–1899	Dan Brouthers, Jimmy Collins, Fred Clarke, Hughie Jennings, Honus Wagner, Rube Waddell
PROVIDENCE GRAYS	1878–1899	Jim O'Rourke, Old Hoss Radbourn, John Ward, George Wright
TROY TROJANS	1879–1882	Dan Brouthers, Roger Connor, Buck Ewing, Tim Keefe, Mickey Welch

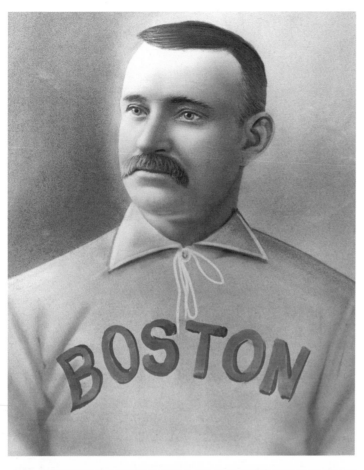

CHARLES RADBOURN

Pitchers in the mid- to late-1800s had little choice but to toss a lot of games and a ton of innings. In fact, "Old Hoss" Radbourn was his team's only pitcher for most of the 1884 season. He won an all-time record 59 games (yes, you read that right) in 678.2 innings (surprisingly, NOT the all-time record). However, even this powerful underarmer met his match with those totals. A solid workhorse before 1884, he pitched for six more seasons, but in none of them did he approach his '84 totals.

AMOS RUSIE

Few Hall of Fame members can boast that they almost single-handedly changed the rules of the game. "The Hoosier Thunderbolt" can, for the most part, lay claim to that title. In 1892, Rusie was on such a strikeout tear that by the next season, everyone was tired of it. For the 1893 National League campaign, the pitcher's mound was moved from its former distance of 50 feet to its current span of 60 feet six inches from home plate. How fast was Rusie? This was in the days before radar guns, of course, but no less an authority than John McGraw claimed that Rusie was the fastest he had ever seen. He put up seasons of 341, 337, and 304 strikeouts in the years leading up to the mound move. Even after the mound backed up, he led the NL three times in strikeouts, while winning more than 30 games twice.

TOP: Charles Radbourn's powerful underarm pitch made him a great asset to his team.
LEFT: Amos Rusie's ability to throw fastballs had a lasting impact on the game.
ABOVE, OPPOSITE: Rube Waddell

Pitching in baseball's early days was a very different proposition from what it is today. Until 1884, for example, pitchers were not allowed to throw from a spot above their waist. Most chose to use a Dan Quisenberry–like submarine motion or a windmill windup much like that in today's fast-pitch softball. There was no elevated mound to help the pitcher "throw downhill," either, although until 1893, the pitcher's "box" was only 50 feet from home plate. In addition, until 1887, batters could request that a pitch be delivered to an area above or below their waist. Missing that batter-chosen zone meant a ball, even if the pitch sailed right over the dish. Add to that the need to pitch almost every day—and just about every inning of every game—and the fact that the ball was often little more than a firm-ish mush by game's end, and you see that pitching was not only different back then, it was harder.

Then there was WILLIAM "CANDY" CUMMINGS (below), who pitched in the pros for only six years (1872–77) but who left an indelible mark. As his Hall of Fame plaque trumpets, he invented the curveball. And batting was never the same after! However, that long-ago innovation aside, comparing pitchers like Cummings, Tim Keefe, "Pud" Galvin, and "Old Hoss" Radbourn to today's players—with their lower pitch and inning counts, modern training techniques, and specialized coaching (to say nothing of the fact that half of them don't have to bat anymore!)—can sometimes seem like apples and oranges. But the basics of the job were the same then as now: figure out a way to get a baseball past a hungry hitter, no matter what the rules or restrictions.

RUBE WADDELL

George Edward Waddell is one of those guys you wish were still pitching today . . . if only for the headlines he'd generate on and off the field. Imagine a blazing pitcher who sets a new all-time single-season mark for strikeouts (as Waddell did in 1904, while leading the league from 1902 through 1907) . . . and who also leaves games in the middle of an inning to chase a passing fire truck. Just Rube being Rube. Imagine a pitcher on his way to winning 27 games in a season who doesn't show up at the ballpark between starts, preferring to spend his time fishing. Imagine the chaos! The headlines! The charm! That was Waddell, one of the flakiest and best pitchers ever. The stories about him have filled several books, but in sum, you could say that Waddell was the dictionary definition of the screwy lefty.

CY YOUNG

You don't get the annual award for the best pitcher in each league named for you without putting up some hellacious numbers. In 22 seasons, Young won a stunning 511 games, one of those records that will never be broken. (In 100-plus years since Young's first season, only a handful of pitchers have come within 150 victories.) He threw the first perfect game of the 1900s in 1904, and he helped the Red Sox win the first World Series in 1903. He had a no-hitter when he was 41. In five seasons, he topped 30 wins and had seven more with 25 or more Ws. Those who played with and against him liked him, a sportsman and a good sport . . . and one of the sport's all-time legends. (By the way, win a trivia contest by knowing that the first Cy Young Award was given in 1955 to Don Newcombe, and that separate Cy Young Awards for each league didn't start until 1967.)

DIZZY DEAN

Everyone's favorite Dean story came when he was taken to the hospital after being whacked in the head by a baseball while sliding into second. The next day's headline: "X-Rays of Dean's Head Reveal Nothing." Like most stories, it exaggerates for effect (it wasn't a headline, it was a quote from Dean), the effect being that Dean was dumb. Not exactly the case. Ol' Diz was not an educated man, but he sure wasn't dumb. And that ol' country boy could pitch, winning 30 games in 1934 as the Cardinals won the World Series. He led the NL four times in strikeouts, including a then-record 17 in a 1933 game. Dean followed his playing career with a popular and country-fun broadcast career.

MARTIN DIHIGO

The Cuban-born Dihigo might be the best all-around player in this book. A star in three countries (add Cuba and Mexico to his years in the Negro Leagues) and a Hall of Famer in all of them, Dihigo excelled as a pitcher, hitter, outfielder, and manager. Today's Cuban players, as they continue to impress international audiences and trickle into the Major Leagues, can look back at Dihigo as a pioneer. His many exploits across the continent, including three Negro League home run titles and 200-plus pitching wins in Mexico and the United States, made him the first Cuban in the Hall of Fame in 1977.

OPPOSITE: *Another one of Cy Young's "unbreakable" records? His career total of 315 losses.*

TOP RIGHT: *Dizzy Dean was a famous combination of personality and pitching prowess.*

RIGHT: *Martin Dihigo's talent as an all-around player is undeniable.*

CHRISTY MATHEWSON

· A GENTLEMAN BASEBALLIST ·

Today's fans—those who visit player websites and line up for hours for autographs, who name their kids for their favorite players and spend thousands of dollars to help train them for a shot at playing in the majors—might be surprised to learn that at the turn of the 20th century, baseball players were considered only slightly above your average blue-collar worker on the American social scale (if that). Those with an education went into the world to make their fortune; those without one might face twelve hours a day in the mines if not playing ball. Pro athletes (essentially just baseball players 'round 1900) were cheered by fans, but would not be invited to dinner.

Christy Mathewson changed all that. Though a handful of "college men" had played pro ball before him, he was the first to combine the upright personal style expected of a gentleman with a fierce competitive spirit and nearly unmatched talent.

His stats are amazing: 12 straight seasons (1903–1914) of 22 or more wins, including four with 30-plus; posting the NL's best ERA and most strikeouts five times each. His 373 wins are tied for third most all-time.

CAREER STATS:	
YEARS:	17
W:	373
L:	188
ERA:	2.13
K:	2,508

Matty's most stunning streak came during the 1905 World Series, when he threw three shutouts for the Giants in six days, allowing only one walk in 27 scoreless innings.

But it was his personality that sets him atop a crowded field of outstanding pitchers of the pre–World War I era. Mathewson conducted himself off the field in such a way that people of the time could point to him as a role model for their kids. He was well spoken, polite, thoughtful, and smart (he covered the World Series as a writer when he wasn't playing in it and authored several books). This was not the general public perception of a ballplayer, and as a result, "Matty" was enormously popular. He was, in some ways, the first real American superstar in the American sport (if you don't count "Cap" and "King").

Like many others in the game, he found himself involved in World War I. While training, he was accidentally gassed, resulting in scars on his lungs. He died in 1925 at the age of only 45. Eleven years later, he was one of two pitchers (Walter Johnson was the other) in the inaugural class of the Baseball Hall of Fame.

CERTIFICATE

In 1951, the Baseball Writers' Association of America named its all-star team for the first 50 years of the 20th century. This certificate recognizes Christy Mathewson's selection to that team.

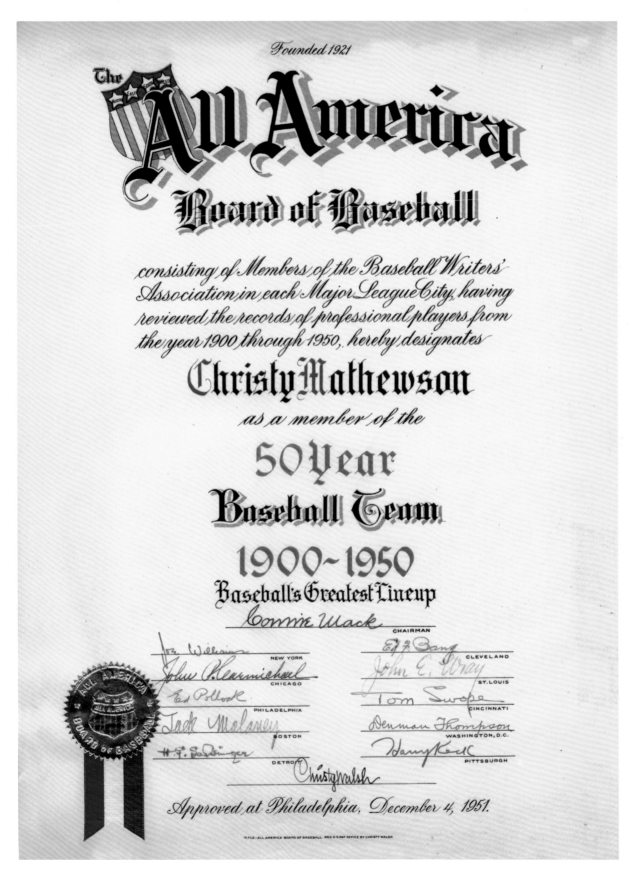

Why Are No Pitchers Called "Righty"?

★ ★ ★

Two outstanding pitchers from this pre- and postwar era (and another from more recent times) boasted a name they earned by dint of their southpaw status. That means they were left-handed, and thus, by baseball tradition, called "Lefty." Left-handed people represent about 13 percent of the general population, but about 25 percent of baseball players. The sport is, in certain respects, one of the few times in life or work that being one of the two possible hands can be an advantage. See Jesse Orosco or any of a number of lefty specialists who had very long careers. How's this for a stat? On baseball-reference.com, a search for "Lefty" turns up 181 players. A search for "Righty"? Zero. Here's a look at a trio of Hall of Fame Leftys.

 ROBERT "LEFTY" GROVE (above) was one of the best pitchers ever. He led the AL in ERA a record nine times; he also earned seven strikeout crowns and had seven straight seasons with 20 or more wins. In an era filled with great hitters (Ruth, Simmons, Gehrig, Foxx, etc.), Grove was still dominant. In 1931, he won 31 games and just about every pitching stat category. No pitcher with 300 wins has as few losses as Grove's 141.

VERNON "LEFTY" GOMEZ earned his fame pitching with some of baseball's best teams behind him. He was part of five Yankees World Series winners in the 1930s, going 6–0 in those Series; he also started four All-Star Games and earned not one but two Triple Crowns.

Turning the page a few years past those two, we find Hall of Famer **STEVE "LEFTY" CARLTON**. While Gomez benefited from great support, Carlton won without it. His 27 wins for the 59-win 1972 Phillies is one of the greatest pitching achievements ever. Carlton won four Cy Young Awards and five NL strikeout crowns.

Other left-handed Hall of Famers Randy Johnson and Tom Glavine were not, for whatever reason, called "Lefty." Of course, Johnson did have one of recent baseball's best nicknames: "The Big Unit."

BOB FELLER

How do you top being a 17-year-old phenom who sets an AL strikeout record in your first month in the bigs? Well, after you go home to finish high school in 1937, you head off on a marvelous baseball journey that lasts more than half a century. "Rapid Robert" built on his boyhood legend with a bat-shattering fastball and a mound intensity rarely seen before or since. He won 20 or more games six times and led the AL in strikeouts seven times, including a career high of 348 in 1946. That latter total was made more remarkable by the fact that he had spent most of the previous four seasons not honing his talents, but firing guns for the Navy. He pitched until 1956, but remained one of baseball's best ambassadors until his death in 2010.

BOB LEMON

After enjoying a cup of coffee in 1941 and 1942 (as a third baseman) and a boatful of the Navy until 1946, the onetime top prospect struggled so much for the Indians that he was almost moved to the outfield. But he made the most of his one more chance, and by 1948, he was a regular in the All-Star Game and a 20-game winner. He helped the Indians reach the World Series twice, and racked up 207 wins, seven seasons with 20 or more wins (more than Feller!), and two wins in two starts during the (winning) 1948 World Series.

HAL NEWHOUSER

Detroit's Prince Hal is the answer to a famous trivia question—name the only pitcher to win back-to-back MVP awards (in 1944 and 1945). In the four seasons after the war, he won 17 or more. He also came in second in the MVP voting in 1946, wrapping up a tremendous three-year run.

TOP LEFT: Bob Feller
TOP RIGHT: Bob Lemon
ABOVE: Hal Newhouser

SATCHEL PAIGE

Many things are believed about the amazing Leroy "Satchel" Paige, but some things are just not "known." Just how old he was, for instance, though most accounts place him at 42 in 1948, when he went 6–1 in relief for the Cleveland Indians. Or whether he did indeed call in his outfield during exhibition games and then strike out the side. Or just how many pitches he had (the "be" ball and the hesitation pitch were known quantities, but others remained a mystery). But amid all the tall tales and varying accounts (many propagated by the publicity-wise Paige), some facts emerge: he was a dominant pitcher in the Negro Leagues and at his height may have been the dominant pitcher in the game. Bob Feller called Satchel "the best pitcher I ever saw." Paige matched up against the best in the majors in postseason exhibitions, and he brought a showmanship to baseball unmatched for the day. Paige's peregrinations through baseball—various Negro League teams, the Dominican Republic, semipro squads of all shapes and sizes, and finally, the majors after the "color line" fell in 1947—took him to diamonds everywhere, but more importantly, to a permanent place in baseball history as one of the best pitchers and most entertaining men ever to step on the field.

ROBIN ROBERTS

Roberts had a bunch of firsts on his Hall of Fame resume. In 1950, he became the first 20-game winner for the Phillies since 1917. That year, he helped the team win an NL pennant. What's more, here's a guy who won 286 games for mostly so-so teams. And as most baseball trivia fans know, Roberts also remains first all-time for most home runs allowed (505), until Jamie Moyer topped him in 2010. Of course, you've got to be pretty good to stick around to set that mark. And you've got to be around the plate, which Roberts' superb fastball often was—he walked fewer than two batters a game for his career.

WILBUR ROGAN

"Bullet Joe" Rogan got his nickname from his first life in the U.S. Army, but built his great baseball career on a wicked curve. Rogan played most often for the Kansas City Monarchs in the Negro National League. His career mark of 116–50 in those games gave him an all-time NNL-best .699 winning percentage. Rogan was also a fine hitter and later a manager and umpire.

TOP: *"Bullet Joe" Rogan had one of baseball's best curveballs.*
LEFT: *Robin Roberts*
OPPOSITE: *Here's Satchel Paige in the uniform of the Kansas City Monarchs.*

• YANKEES GREATS •

The Bronx Bombers have gotten a lot of attention for a hit parade of sluggers, but they also boasted some of the greatest arms of all time. This trio of Hall of Famers from the years before and after World War II, plus Lefty Gomez, represent a century of Yankees hurlers.

WAITE HOYT was the man on the mound for the 1920s Yankees who were led on offense by a guy named Babe. A crafty right-hander who had terrific control, Hoyt pitched in six World Series for the Bombers; the team won three.

RED RUFFING caught fire when he moved from the Red Sox to the Yankees in 1930. He lowered his career-best ERA three times during his decade with the Yankees. He also helped New York win six World Series, winning seven Series games himself and pitching (with a two-year stint in the Army) until 1946.

WHITEY FORD (right) was the third in this series of Yankees aces. "The Chairman of the Board" was a crafty lefty if there ever was one, calmly using an array of pitches to win 236 games against only 106 losses, the best percentage in the 1900s after Spud Chandler's. He still holds World Series career records with 10 wins and 94 strikeouts.

HILTON SMITH

Satchel Paige cast a pretty large shadow on the Kansas City Monarchs, but Smith's light shined through nonetheless. Often hidden in the headline-making glare of the mighty Satch, Smith won at least 20 games in 12 seasons, including a stunning 11–1 mark in 1941.

WARREN SPAHN

While few ever really called him "Lefty" (see box on page 22), Warren Spahn was the winningest left-handed pitcher of all time (363 wins). Spahn pitched and pitched and pitched, starting in 1946 at age 25, following World War II service, and sticking around until 1965. But his greatest years were in the 1950s with the Braves, when he led the NL in wins five straight years (1957–1961); he had also led in three earlier seasons. His last victory title came in 1961, when he was 40 years old. He also won the ERA title that season. At points in his career, he won at least three season titles in wins, strikeouts, ERA, complete games, shutouts, and innings pitched. He also set the NL record for pitchers with 35 career home runs.

TOP RIGHT: *Warren Spahn demonstrates a big-kick windup.*

TOP LEFT, ABOVE: **Hilton Smith**

BASEBALL, THE HALL, AND THE WAR

"Rapid Robert" Feller was just one of hundreds of baseball players who served in World War II. A Navy man, Feller missed nearly four seasons in the prime of his career and never regretted it for a second. Ted Williams went from being an MVP in 1942 to becoming an Army Air Corps pilot in 1943 (and he returned to fly again in the Korean War). Hank Greenberg signed up even before Pearl Harbor. Yogi Berra, Joe DiMaggio, Bobby Doerr, Mickey Cochrane, Warren Spahn, and Pee Wee Reese are among the many Hall of Famers who put aside their gloves and picked up whatever arms Uncle Sam gave them (which in many cases was another glove, but they played for service teams and not for big-league glory). The game played on throughout the war, but it was without some of the star power it enjoyed before and after.

THE WHITE HOUSE
WASHINGTON

January 15, 1942.

My dear Judge:-

Thank you for yours of January fourteenth. As you will, of course, realize the final decision about the baseball season must rest with you and the Baseball Club owners -- so what I am going to say is solely a personal and not an official point of view.

I honestly feel that it would be best for the country to keep baseball going. There will be fewer people unemployed and everybody will work longer hours and harder than ever before.

And that means that they ought to have a chance for recreation and for taking their minds off their work even more than before.

Baseball provides a recreation which does not last over two hours or two hours and a half, and which can be got for very little cost. And, incidentally, I hope that night games can be extended because it gives an opportunity to the day shift to see a game occasionally.

As to the players themselves, I know you agree with me that individual players who are of active military or naval age should go, without question, into the services. Even if the actual quality of the teams is lowered by the greater use of older players, this will not dampen the popularity of the sport. Of course, if any individual has some particular aptitude in a trade or profession, he ought to serve the Government. That, however, is a matter which I know you can handle with complete justice.

Here is another way of looking at it -- if 300 teams use 5,000 or 6,000 players, these players are a definite recreational asset to at least 20,000,000 of their fellow citizens -- and that in my judgment is thoroughly worthwhile.

With every best wish,

Very sincerely yours,

Franklin D. Roosevelt

Hon. Kenesaw M. Landis,
333 North Michigan Avenue,
Chicago,
Illinois.

BERT BLYLEVEN

This curveball specialist had to cross an ocean to reach Cooperstown. Rik Aalbert Blyleven became the first player born in the Netherlands to reach the Hall of Fame. The road to his plaque was almost as long as the trip to America, as Blyleven retired in 1992, but was not elected until 2011. Blyleven was just 19 in 1970 when he pitched his first full season, winning 10 games for the Twins, the first of 10 straight 10-win seasons. After two years with Texas, he joined Pittsburgh and won a game in the Pirates' World Series triumph. He got his second Fall Classic win back with Minnesota in 1987. Never a mega-star, but nearly always a winner, Blyleven's 22-year career ended at the Hall of Fame.

JIM BUNNING

This powerful right-hander was the first player to do the following in both the American and National Leagues: win 100 games, record 1,000 strikeouts, pitch in an All-Star Game, and toss a no-hitter. His NL no-hitter was a career-capper, though, since it was perfect (see page 50). He was later elected governor of Kentucky and retired as that state's Republican U.S. senator in 2010. Bunning passed away in 2017.

*BELOW LEFT: **Burt Blyleven***
*BELOW RIGHT: **Jim Bunning***

SANDY KOUFAX

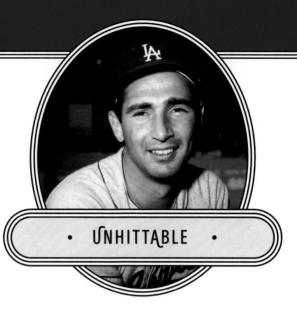

• UNHITTABLE •

In 1957, Sandy Koufax was not Sandy Koufax. He was a lefty who looked like he was on his way to a short, journeyman-like career. But a couple of years later, almost suddenly, Sandy Koufax became Sandy Koufax.

His story was the tale of two pitchers. Koufax started his career in 1955 and struggled through six mediocre seasons, never topping 11 wins and once leading the NL in wild pitches. His speed kept him in business; in a 1959 game, he tied a record with 18 strikeouts. Something was happening, and in 1961 it happened for good. Somehow, the serious-minded, fireballing lefty from Brooklyn found his touch. For the next six seasons, almost no one could touch him.

Koufax's amazing run from 1961–1966 remains a period of almost unmatched pitching brilliance. The numbers tell one part of the story: five straight ERA titles, four strikeout crowns, three Cy Young Awards, three seasons with 25-plus wins, and four no-hitters, the last, in 1965, a perfect game.

But the attitude of those who faced his invisible fastball and neck-snapping curve tells another part of the story. Former batting champ Harvey Kuenn got this brief report from teammate

Joe Amalfitano as Kuenn went to the plate to try to break up Koufax's perfect game: "Harvey, you might as well not bother going up there." It was not so much fear that held opponents in thrall (Koufax had pitch-'em-inside teammate Don Drysdale to give them that), it was awe. Everyone knew what was coming . . . but no one could stop it. Even foreknowledge didn't help. Historian Paul Dickson points out that by 1963, the whole NL knew how Koufax tipped his pitches, but it just didn't matter. He was unhittable.

He led the Dodgers to World Series wins in 1963 and 1965. They won another pennant in 1966, but Koufax lost his only appearance against the Orioles in that Series. And that, suddenly, was that. The pain from ongoing arthritis, pain he had managed for several years with ice and guts, was too much. At the age of 30, Sandy Koufax was done, retired due to injury. In 1972, he became the youngest man ever elected to the Hall of Fame. He worked briefly as a broadcaster, but in the years since he has become more of a ghost, accessible to a few friends and an occasional Dodgers instructor, but never a media presence. Never on the banquet circuit. And in his mystery, the majesty of his talent continues to speak for himself.

CAREER STATS:

YEARS:	12
W:	165
L:	87
ERA:	2.76
K:	2,396

OPPOSTIE: *Sandy Koufax's career was not as long as others, but it shined brightly.*

ABOVE: *Sandy Koufax takes aim.*

SCOUT REPORT CARD

This scouting report for "pitcher-first baseman" Sandy Koufax,
written in 1954, gives him an "A+" arm.

Player should fill out this side only — please print.—

Position _P._

Name _KOUFAX_   _SANFORD_   Bats _R._
      (Last)   (First)   Throws _L._

Address _1104   83RD ST.   BROOKLYN   28, N.Y._
         (Street & No.)   (City & State)

Date of Birth _DEC.   30   1935_   Height _6'2"_ Weight _200_
        (Month)   (Day)   (Year)

Parent's name _EVELYN — IRVING   KOUFAX_

Parent's address _SAME AS ABOVE_   Telephone _TE. 74415_

Date High School Class Graduates(d) _JUNE   1   1953_
                             (Month)   (Day)   (Year)

Have you ever signed a professional baseball contract _No_

If so, when ___

With what club ___

List any other Clubs with which you have played ___

Date _MAY 15, 1954_

SCOUT REPORT CARD

Name in Full _SANFORD   KOUFAX_   Pos. _P-1st._ Age _18_

                                          Hgt. _6'2"_ Wgt. _200_

Club _UNIV. — CINCINNATI_   League _IND._   Bats _R._ Throws _L._

Arm _A+_   Accuracy _A-_

Fielding _A-_

Hitting _A-_   Power _A-_

Running Speed _O+_   Base Running _—_

PITCHER		
Speed	_A_	VERY GOOD PROSPECT, ALSO
Curve	_A-_	VERY GOOD HITTER. HAS
Change	_A-_	AVERAGED 16 STRIKE OUTS
Control	_A-_	PER GAME, THIS SEASON.

APTITUDE _VERY GOOD_

Aggressiveness _OUT-STANDING_

Definite Prospect? _✓_   Has Chance?   Habits

Physical Description (Build, Size, Agility, Etc.) _TALL — MUSCULAR — QUICK_
REFLEXES, WELL COORDINATED

Other Remarks: _GOING TO U. OF CINCINNATI, ON SCHOLARSHIP_
NOT INTERESTED IN PRO. BALL UNTIL HE GRADUATE

Report By _BILL — ZINSER_   Date _MAY 15, 1954_

Note: This card to be used in reporting ALL PLAYERS in Brooklyn organization and any PROSPECTS
outside Brooklyn organization.

ALSO PLAYS 1ST. BECAUSE OF HITTING ABILITY

LIKE AN EGG

Pitchers combine arm motion, body motion, and grip to make their pitching magic. While each pitcher has his own quirks, there are some standard ways that they hold the baseball. Grab a ball and see if you can hold a ball these ways. Just don't try to throw any of them past Wade Boggs.

TWO-SEAM FASTBALL
The name comes from the position of the first two fingers along the seams at their narrowest point. Arm motion can impart slight sinking or "running in" motion.

FOUR-SEAM FASTBALL
The classic power pitch, it gets backspin when released off the fingers, while arm speed provides the power to make it the fastest of the fastballs.

CURVEBALL
Two fingers grip one of the seams and use the traction gained to give the ball spin, aided by a twist of the wrist upon release. A great curveball can buckle knees and reduce hitters to jelly.

SLIDER
Another breaking pitch, it has more side-to-side motion than the sweeping or sharp-breaking curveball. It also moves faster, more like a fastball. At release, the wrist turns like opening a doorknob.

KNUCKLEBALL
It should be called a fingernail ball, since that's what actually grips the ball. It is released straight ahead out of a grip like this one. The lack of spin means that it can bob and weave erratically plateward.

STEVE CARLTON

How's this for typical Steve Carlton? In 1969, he set a then-record by striking out 19 Mets … and the Cardinals lost the game 4–3. In 1972, he won 27 games for the Phillies; the other Philly hurlers won 32—combined. The talent of this four-time Cy Young Award–winner finally paid off with a ring in 1980 as he won 24 games and led the Phillies to their first World Series championship. "Lefty" was known not only for his pitching prowess, but his ground-breaking training routines, including newfangled hand workouts, mental visualization techniques, and constant physical training.

DON DRYSDALE

Don Drysdale was baseball's most jealous landlord. He protected the land he felt was his—home plate—with a ferocity that made him both feared and respected. Drysdale was an old-school pitcher in a time of great change: the 1960s. But he was more than a batter-buzzer. He put together a record string of 58 2/3 scoreless innings in 1968. After his retirement in 1969, he became a popular broadcaster.

TOP: Don Drysdale teamed with Sandy Koufax to help the Dodgers win three World Series.
LEFT, ABOVE: Steve "Lefty" Carlton was all right for the Phillies, helping them win the longtime franchise's first World Series in 1980.

BOB GIBSON

In 1968, the "Year of the Pitcher," Bob Gibson was the king of the mound. That was nothing new for the Cardinals' ace, among the best right-handed pitchers of the decade. Though he was already a World Series hero (his career total of eight Series wins is second most), having led St. Louis to titles in 1964 and 1967, Gibson's '68 campaign was what set him apart. His 1.12 ERA was the third-best in the 20th century. He gave up one run after throwing five straight shutouts, then reeled off another 17 scoreless innings. In one 95-inning stretch, the man who had overcome a series of serious childhood illnesses gave up but two earned runs. The amazing thing about 1968, in which he threw 13 shutouts—a great career for pitchers today—is that he managed to lose nine games! Big, strong, athletic (he played hoops in school and had a stint with the Harlem Globetrotters), Gibson was a mighty force on the mound, unafraid to pitch inside and a terror to hitters and catchers alike.

TOM GLAVINE

This crafty lefty also spent 22 seasons in the bigs, earning ten All-Star bids and a pair of Cy Young Awards. Each of his five 20-win seasons with Atlanta led the NL. Glavine was a key part of the great Braves pitching staff that helped Atlanta win 14 straight NL East titles. In 1995, the Braves finally broke through with a World Series triumph. Glavine won Game Two and the clinching Game Six, allowing only two earned runs in 14 innings. He got a World Series ring and was named the Series MVP. The postseason was nothing new to Glavine; he pitched in 24 different series, starting 35 games. He earned his 300th career win while with the Mets in 2007 at the age of 41.

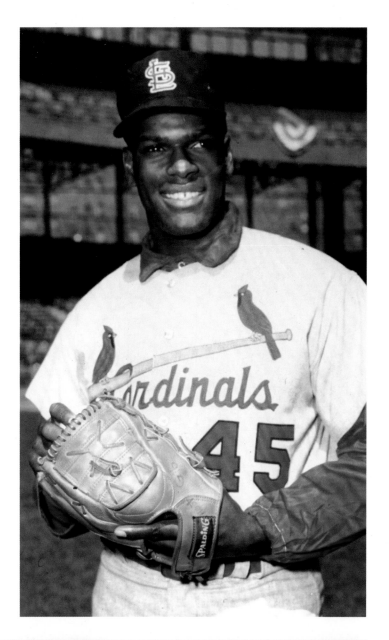

OPPOSITE AND TOP:
Bob Gibson was famous for "flying off" the mound after his delivery.
RIGHT: Tom Glavine

Here Come the Firemen

Until the 1970s, pitchers were, for the most part, expected to finish what they started. Relief pitchers were failed starters—mop-up men. The specialization of relief work grew slowly to include aces like Roy Face, Mike Marshall, Jim Konstanty, and Kent Tekulve.

The first nearly full-time relief pitcher to earn a spot in the Hall was **HOYT WILHELM**. In a 21-year career with nine teams, he was a full-time starter only once (1959 with Baltimore). Otherwise, the rubber-armed knuckleball specialist appeared in 40-plus games in all but a handful of seasons. When he retired in 1972, his 1,070 appearances were an all-time record.

Very slightly overlapping Wilhelm and carrying the torch of relief pitcher further up the mountain was Hall of Famer **ROLLIE FINGERS**. He helped the A's win three straight World Series, racking up six saves in those championships. Although far from being a one-inning save artist, Fingers was the best of his generation, capping off his career with a Cy Young Award/MVP double-dip in 1981 with the Brewers.

DENNIS ECKERSLEY switched from being a pretty good starter to an unhittable closer. He matched Fingers's double awards in 1992 with a remarkable 7–1 record, 51 saves, and a 1.91 ERA. Eck's sidewinding delivery and mound swagger made him the standard for the modern closer. His amazing control was an even bigger asset.

BRUCE SUTTER was not the colorful personality that Eck was, but he was nearly as effective. He led the NL in saves five times with a devastating split-finger fastball that sank wickedly. He joined Eck in the Hall in 2006.

RICH "GOOSE" GOSSAGE met the relief pitcher Hall of Fame standard and become the fourth modern closer in Cooperstown in 2008. A two-time AL saves leader, his main weapons were a powerful fastball and a style that just about dared the opponents to beat him . . . at their peril.

The rise of the relievers sets the stage for others to join this elite crew in the future.

ROY HALLADAY

As the complete game became a remnant of baseball's past, Halladay remained a modern master. The big righty led either league in CGs seven times. He is one of the few players to earn a Cy Young Award in each league (2003 with Toronto and 2010 with Philadelphia) and was an eight-time All-Star. Though he never made the World Series, he owns a place in postseason history. He threw a no-hitter, allowing a single walk, in Game One of the NLDS against Cincinnati. It is the only no-no after the regular season except for Don Larsen's 1956 World Series perfect game. Halladay retired in 2013 and, sadly, died in a small-plane accident in 2017. He was inducted into the Hall two years later.

JIM HUNTER

Say "Jim Hunter" to most baseball fans and you'll probably get a blank look. But simply say "Catfish" and you'll get smiles and nods all around. Hunter can thank A's owner Charlie Finley for creating that famous nickname, but he had only his skills and tenacity to thank for a Hall of Fame career. Along with the new moniker, the highlights of his Oakland days were a 1968 perfect game and three straight World Series titles. For today's ballplayers, the highlight of Hunter's career was his 1974 appeal to baseball's arbitrator, who made him the first true free agent in baseball. His 1974 contract with the Yankees gave him the first $1 million signing bonus and opened the floodgates. Hunter made New York's money good by helping them win the 1977 and 1978 World Series.

ABOVE: *Jim Hunter was part of three World Series champs in Oakland.*
BELOW: *Roy Halladay, who had the first postseason no-hitter since 1956.*

RANDY JOHNSON

For the first part of his career, the tall lefty known as the "Big Unit" should have been called "Wild Thing." Johnson showed great promise and great power, but he couldn't be shown the strike zone, leading the AL in walks three straight years. He eventually solved his problems, and rarely walked more than 100 batters in a season again. He began a run of four straight AL strikeout totals, too. By 1995, he was the AL Cy Young Award winner and the dominant pitcher in the game. After signing with Arizona in 1999, he got even better, winning four straight Cy Youngs with four seasons of 330-Ks plus, including a stunning high of 372, one of the all-time marks. The capper was the 2001 season in which he was the World Series co-MVP after he started and won Games Two and Six and won Game Seven in relief. Good thing he found the strike zone all those years ago!

GREG MADDUX

In the pantheon of greatest pitchers of all time, Maddux the Professor clearly owns a spot. The righty was one of only two players with four straight Cy Young Awards (1992–95), won four NL ERA titles, a trio of NL win titles, and a legion of frustrated opponents. He won the first Cy Young in the last of his first set of seasons with the Cubs and the next three with Atlanta, for whom he pitched 11 years. Never an overpowering pitcher, his control was legendary. Maddux owned the strike zone no matter who was hitting. He helped himself with his glove, too, winning an incredible 18 Gold Gloves, the last coming when he was 42 with the Dodgers and Padres. After all that, no wonder he entered the Hall on a stunning 97.2 percent of the ballots.

*BELOW: **Greg Maddux***
*OPPOSITE: **Randy Johnson***

JUAN MARICHAL

What a leg kick! What a fastball! It was Marichal's misfortune to be one of baseball's best pitchers in an era with a slew of such hurlers. He had more wins than Bob Gibson every year in the 1960s and topped the NL in wins in 1963 during Sandy Koufax's stunning run. Yet Marichal never won the Cy Young Award. In 1968, known as the Year of the Pitcher, he led the NL with 26 wins. The first Dominican player to achieve lasting big-league success, Marichal baffled hitters with a high-kicking delivery that is still among baseball's most memorable. To say nothing of the wide array of pitches, speeds, and the pinpoint control that made him truly great.

TOP: *Juan Marichal demonstrates the start of his famous high leg kick.*
OPPOSITE: *Pedro Martínez*

PEDRO MARTÍNEZ

Martínez will forever be a hero in Boston for helping the Red Sox break the "Curse of the Bambino" in 2004, when the righty was 16-9 and won Game Three in the World Series. That was one of many highlights for this native of the Dominican Republic. He won his first Cy Young Award with Montreal in 1997 with a sparkling 1.90 ERA. Amazingly, he then improved after moving to the Red Sox. In 1999, he won the pitching Triple Crown and his second Cy Young. He made it two in a row in 2000, when his 1.74 ERA was the second-lowest since 1968. Martínez featured a great fastball, with a devastating split-finger pitch and a nasty curve. With Montreal in 1995, he threw nine perfect innings in a game, but the Expos didn't score and he lost the perfecto and the game in the tenth. It was a rare disappointment for one of baseball's all-time hurlers.

JACK MORRIS

Some players shine brightest in the biggest games. That was Morris. He won both of his WS starts with the Tigers as they won the 1984 World Series. He earned his ring in the 1991 Series cementing his big-game legend. After winning the opener, he came back to throw a 10-inning shutout in Game Seven. He gutted out the final innings, shaking off any attempt to pull him out. He added a third World Series win with the Blue Jays in 1992. Morris was not too shabby in the regular season, either, using a bat-missing split-fingered fastball to lead the Majors in the 1980s with 162 wins.

MIKE MUSSINA

Steady excellence was the hallmark of Mussina's long career. He pitched for the Orioles for 10 seasons and won 147 games, yet only made six postseason starts. When he joined the Yankees in 2001, he got a chance to shine in the playoffs and made 21 starts in 12 post-season series. Mussina saved his best for last, winning a career-best 20 games in his final season in 2008 to wrap up a 270-win career. In fact, Mussina had only one losing season in 17 full seasons as a starter.

TOP: *Jack Morris*
BELOW: *Mike Mussina*

PHIL NIEKRO

Niekro led the NL in losses four times and in hits allowed in three seasons. He gave up more homers than any other NL pitcher four times. And he lost 274 games. But his longevity and perseverance (and 318 wins) were rewarded with a trip to the Hall. In his 24 seasons of floating up tantalizing knuckleballs, Niekro topped 20 wins three times and had 13 winning seasons (in 1979, he led the NL with 21 wins . . . and 20 losses!).

JIM PALMER

Palmer was so consistently good that he sometimes escapes notice when the talk comes around to all-time greats. A three-time Cy Young winner and eight-time 20-game winner, Palmer's 10-year run from 1969 to 1978 was practically boring in its sustained excellence. He also helped the Orioles reach six World Series, including two championships. His 1975 season was his best: 23 wins, including 10 shutouts, a league-best 2.09 ERA, and his second Cy Young Award.

*TOP: **Phil Niekro***
*BELOW AND RIGHT: **Jim Palmer used his long,***
lean form to generate surprising power.

MARIANO RIVERA

· SUPER SAVER ·

There are more than 330 members of the Baseball Hall of Fame. All of them went through an election process to earn their spot. And among all of those legends, heroes, superstars, and giants only one—one!—has been elected unanimously. Mariano Rivera earned that unique distinction with a magnificent career as the preeminent closer in the game's history. His 652 career saves are most all-time, while his postseason 0.70 ERA will probably remain unmatched for a long time. He had nine seasons with 40 or more saves, including 44 in his final season of 2013.

Rivera was blessed with two things: long, pliable fingers that allowed him to throw his untouchable cut fastball, and an innate desire to succeed both as a player and as a person. In 19 seasons, he was the personification of excellence on the mound, always coming through for his team but also deflecting praise with humility. He was a 13-time All-Star, earning the game's MVP award in 2013 on his way to Cooperstown.

His Yankee teams won five World Series, with Rivera at the heart of all of them. Rivera pitched in 96 postseason games and had saves (42) in nearly half of them.

Hall of Fame voters are experts and they know greatness when they see it. They're also human, and it was Rivera's remarkable calm, thoughtfulness, and consideration that truly put him in a class by himself—Mr. 100 Percent.

CAREER STATS:	
YEARS:	19
W:	82
SAVES:	652
ERA:	2.21
K:	1,173

*ABOVE: **Mariano Rivera on the hill.***

RIVERA'S CAREER HIGHLIGHT UNIFORMS

Below, Mariano Rivera's New York Yankees home jersey worn during the 2008 All-Star Game at Yankee Stadium. The black armband was added in memory of Bobby Murcer. Bottom right, the cap Rivera wore at his last All-Star Game. Bottom left, Rivera's shoes from the 1999 World Series where he was named Series MVP.

GAYLORD PERRY

Whether you think Perry "doctored" the baseball (as was long alleged) or not, his career-long mind game with hitters obscured the fact that the guy could pitch. He won a Cy Young Award in each league, led a league three times in wins, and topped 20 wins five times in a 22-year career in which he wore the caps of eight teams. Along with his winning ways came a unique set of pre-pitch gyrations—designed to both confuse hitters and obfuscate umpires—that made him the "stuff" of legend.

NOLAN RYAN

No pitcher has ever thrown for as many seasons, recorded as many strikeouts, issued as many walks, or tossed as many no-hitters as the great Nolan Ryan. The very epitome of the power pitcher, Ryan survived early-career wildness (he was an eight-time league leader in walks) to become the dominant power pitcher of the second half of the 20th century. He led his league in strikeouts an amazing 11 times, including an all-time high of 383 in 1973. He played well beyond the usual effective age for pitchers, adding his seventh no-hitter (no one else has more than four) when he was 44 years old. Stick around that long and you end up as the third-losingest pitcher ever, but you also reach 324 wins and take a Ryan Express trip to Cooperstown.

ABOVE: *Gaylord Perry*
OPPOSITE: *No one pitched in more Major League seasons than Nolan Ryan.*

PERFECT

★ Twenty-three men have thrown perfect games in the majors since 1880. Only eight are in the Hall of Fame, including Randy Johnson, who was the oldest to hurl a perfecto when he did the deed in 2004. John Ward was the second to reach perfection, only five days after the first in 1880. Twenty-four years later, Cy Young blanked the Athletics to add another chapter to his remarkable career. Addie Joss was perfect in 1908. We then leap all the way to 1964 when future Kentucky senator Jim Bunning got 27 straight vs. the Mets. Bunning accomplished his feat on Father's Day, fitting for a man with nine kids! The next year, Sandy Koufax (page 30) was perfect in his then-record fourth career no-hitter. Catfish Hunter joined the Hall of Fame perfect club in 1968 by knocking off the Twins, and Roy Halladay was perfect for the Phillies in 2010, cementing his Cooperstown credentials.

You don't have to be perfect to get into the Hall of Fame . . . but it doesn't hurt!

Record-Setting Closers

★ ★ ★

In the 21st century, the role of the closer—the one-inning wonder who shuts teams down for the win—has become cemented as part of baseball strategy. Among the crowd of intimidating pitchers who filled that role, two stood out for longevity and steady success.

LEE SMITH (above left) stood 6'5" and looked even taller and more fierce as he eyed each batter. He racked up at least 30 saves in 10 seasons, including a career-high 47 in 1991, one of four times he led his league in the stat. Smith took over the career saves lead in 1993, ending his career with 478.

Records were made to be broken, however, and 13 years later, **TREVOR HOFFMAN** (above right) notched save No. 479. Hoffman didn't blow hitters away; instead, his changeup left them looking foolish. Pitching for the Padres for 16 seasons (plus three more among the Brewers and Marlins), he was a bright light on some underwhelming teams. He amassed a then-record 601 saves. The NL reliever of the year is now given the Trevor Hoffman Award.

JOHN SMOLTZ

Smoltzie is the rare pitcher with great success as a starter and closer. As a starter with Atlanta from 1988 to 1999, he was a consistent winner and a two-time NL strikeout king, with his best season coming in 1996 when he led MLB with 24 wins and won the NL Cy Young. Following an injury that kept him out of the 2000 season, he returned as a closer. He was dominant, leading the NL with 55 saves in 2002 and topping 44 saves in the next two seasons. Having proved he could do that, he moved back to the rotation and led the NL in wins in 2006. He was clutch when it counted, posting a remarkable 15–4 postseason record, including a perfect 7-0 in NLDS games.

TOM SEAVER

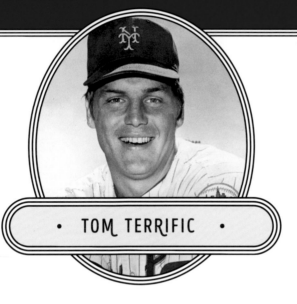

• TOM TERRIFIC •

CAREER STATS:

YEARS:	20
W:	311
L:	205
ERA:	2.86
K:	3,640

Rookie of the Year in 1967. Three Cy Young Awards. Three ERA and five strikeout titles. Carried the Mets to their first world championship in 1969. Sixteen out of 20 seasons with a winning record. A then-record-tying 19 strikeouts in a 1970 game. When elected to the Hall of Fame in 1992, he received the highest percentage of votes ever: 98.8 percent.

That's the capsule biography of the man they called "Tom Terrific," but the stats and awards don't do justice to the man or even the player. As evidenced by his Hall of Fame votes, he was and is beloved in the game. Respected as a competitor, Seaver is a modern exemplar of the rare combination of greatness of body and spirit. From his earliest days in the bigs, he was thought of as combining maturity with his innate skills. And some skills they were: a

whomping fastball urged plateward with a pistonlike power, not to mention his devastating slider. Add good control (he averaged about 2.6 walks per nine innings) and an almost insane will to win, and you have got a recipe for greatness. He arrived on the Mets with the team mired in mediocrity; he left them—traded by a grumpy and shortsighted management—in 1977 as two-time NL champs and first-time World Champs. His pitching was one way he led; his uncompromising focus on winning was another.

Earlier, we focused on Christy Mathewson, the first example of the ballplayer as gentleman and role model. In Tom Terrific, baseball and its fans enjoyed another.

OPPOSITE: Gotham ace Tom Seaver helped the Mets win it all in 1969 and led them to another NL pennant in 1973.

2

THE CATCHERS

They play what's arguably baseball's toughest position. They get nicked by foul balls, whacked by bats, dinged by pitches in the dirt, and bowled over by charging base runners. After all this, they are expected to dust themselves off and then become hitters just moments later. And of course, there's all that squatting.

Catchers have long seemed like the ditchdiggers of baseball—hard-working, hidden from view behind a mask, perennially dirty. Yet they play, as any expert will tell you, the most important defensive position on the field. From calling pitches to helping calm emotional pitchers, from controlling the opponents' running game to preventing runs at the plate, catchers are involved in more pitches than any other player. Yet try to get your average Little League parent to put their kid behind the plate . . .

As a testament to the difficulty and challenge of the job, catchers are the second-least-represented (after third basemen) fielding position in the Hall of Fame. Still, as the great Casey Stengel famously said, upon drafting a catcher with first pick in the 1962 expansion draft, "You gotta have a catcher. Otherwise, you are going to have a lot of passed balls."

OPPOSITE: Catcher Gordon "Mickey" Cochrane crouches at the ready.

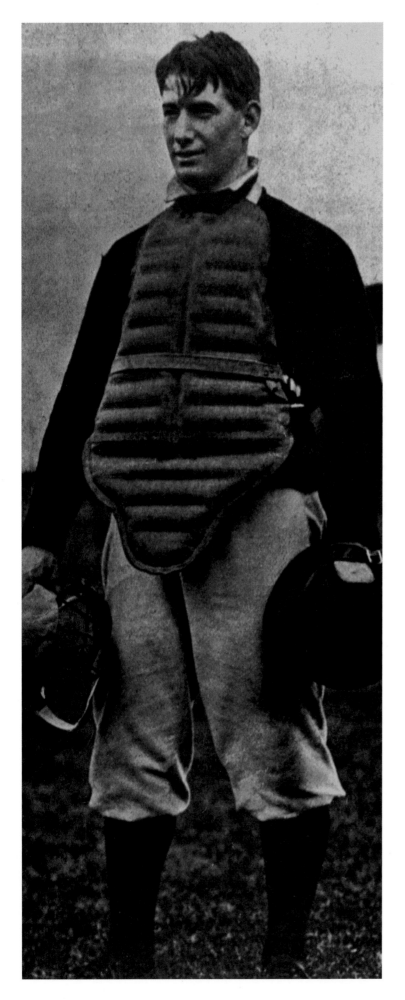

CATCHING PIONEERS

Men had been playing baseball's toughest position for about 80 years, so there was a big collection to choose from. But when the Hall of Fame chose its first catcher, it chose **WILLIAM "BUCK" EWING**, who had last played the position in 1893. However, for the decade of the 1880s, Ewing was not only the best catcher, he was also one of the best all-around players.

The second catcher in the Hall actually came to his trade later in his career. After starting as a pitcher and outfielder, **ROGER BRESNAHAN** squatted down for good in 1905. His ability to handle great Giants pitchers like Christy Mathewson and "Iron Man" Joe McGinnity made him the exemplar for catchers to follow. His creative solution to a perennial catchers' problem (shin guards) also helped secure his legend.

TOP: William "Buck" Ewing shows off the uniform of his era.
LEFT: Roger Bresnahan captured in a time before he invented shin guards.

SOUVENIR TICKET

Fans at Ebbets Field received this special 1940 Opening Day souvenir ticket. Note that the catcher's mitt design does not have the modern hinge, which was not introduced until the late 1960s.

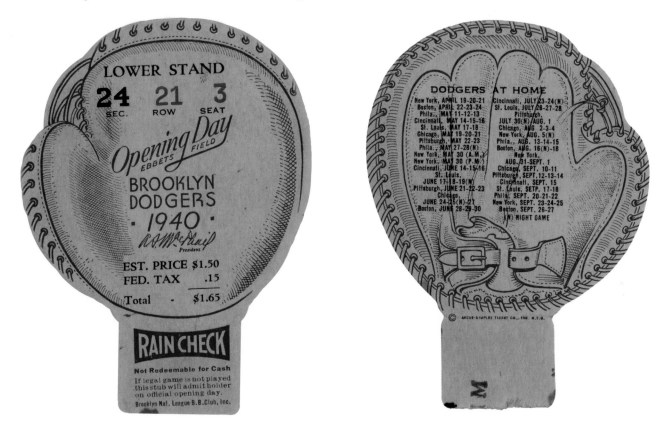

BASEBALL CARD

Roger Bresnahan established his Hall-of-Fame credentials with the Giants before spending 1909–1912 with the Cardinals.

 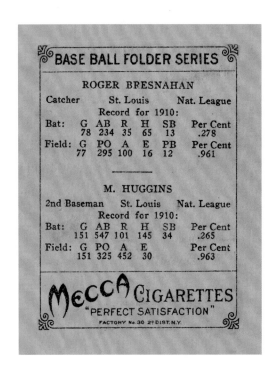

Another catcher from the World War I era who joined the Hall in 1955 is perhaps best remembered for one of his lowest moments. **RAY SCHALK** was the catcher on the ill-fated 1919 Black Sox team; he was not implicated in the scheme, however. Far from a slugger (he had more than two homers in only one of his 18 seasons), Schalk was an outstanding defensive catcher and handler of pitchers. He caught a record four no-hitters.

BELOW: Ray Schalk's dreams of a World Series win in 1919 fell to the Black Sox scandal.
OPPOSITE: The Thayer mask was much rounder and with larger holes than today's better-fitting models.

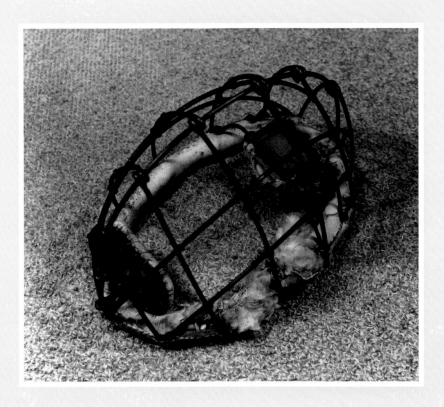

Thank You, Fred

For the first quarter-century of what we now recognize as organized baseball, catchers got clobbered. They wore no extra protective gear. Even though they were often positioned numerous feet behind the batter and caught pitches on one bounce, they still were nicked, knocked, and clipped. In 1876, a Harvard man named **FRED THAYER** rebuilt a fencing mask to protect his team's catcher, James Tyng. The cage-like mask gradually evolved into today's full-head plastic-and-metal helmet.

The chest protector has a less specific history, but came along a bit after the mask. The first were worn underneath the uniform shirt, perhaps to help avoid teasing from opponents. Baseball players were expected to be tough guys, after all. By the turn of the century, they were outside the jersey and getting larger, thicker, and longer, made of cloth, leather, and stuffing.

Shin guards didn't make their first appearance until 1907, and it took the courage of a future Hall of Famer to earn them due respect. Roger Bresnahan modified guards worn in cricket to protect his lower legs. After dealing with some initial joshing, Bresnahan proved prescient and soon all catchers wore the leather covers.

From a state of being the same as the other eight players, catchers have evolved into the best-protected players on the field, shoving aside the jeers of their use of the "tools of ignorance."

CATCHERS BECOME HITTERS

The offensive outburst that infected baseball beginning in 1920 affected several catchers. From the era between the wars comes a trio of some of the best hitting catchers of all time.

GABBY HARTNETT had good timing. He showed up ready to hit, and the still-new "lively ball" was ready to be hit. He became the first catcher in baseball history to notch 1,000 RBI and 200 homers, and put together a .297 career batting average. The offense was nice, but he would have been a star for defense alone. He led NL catchers in fielding percentage and assists six times each. The only reason he was on just six All-Star teams is that the game didn't start until 1933, when he was 32 years old. The 1935 MVP, Hartnett is well-remembered for hitting the "Homer in the Gloamin'," a late-inning, NL pennant-winning homer for the Cubs in 1938.

MICKEY COCHRANE was one of baseball's best all-around catchers. Cochrane's career .320 batting average is still the best ever for a catcher. He was also a great backstop and fiery leader, first for Connie Mack's great Athletic teams in the late 1920s. The Detroit Tigers traded for him from the Athletics for a player, and cash, after the 1933 season and made him the player-manager—and Detroit won the pennant in 1934 and '35. Ironically, for a guy who made his living in baseball's trenches, Cochrane was hurt as a batter. A beaning in 1937 effectively ended the Hall of Fame career of "Black Mike."

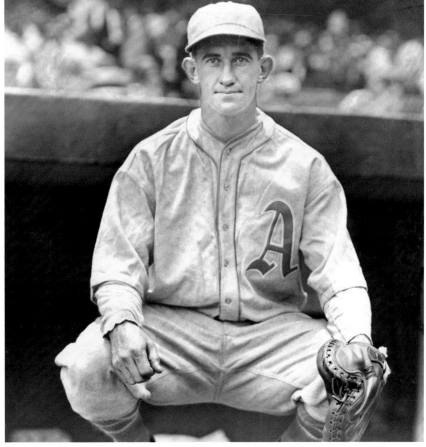

TOP: Gabby Hartnett was a Cub for 19 years.
LEFT: Mickey Cochrane

It's too bad that **ERNIE LOMBARDI** is usually included in stories about famous noses; he deserves a better run in stories about great ballplayers. The man known for obvious reasons as "Schnozz" was one of the best-hitting catchers ever. Until 2006, Lombardi was the last catcher to lead a league in batting average (1938, when he was MVP, and 1942). His .306 career average might have been higher had he not also been perhaps the slowest person in big-league history.

RIGHT: Ernie Lombardi was a two-time batting champ.
BELOW: Mickey Cochrane

STARS IN–AND OUT OF–THE SHADOWS

When experts are putting together their "all-time" lists of the greatest players at each position, the stars of the Negro League often get short shrift. However, one of their number nearly always finds his way into the mix. **JOSH GIBSON** just might have been the greatest slugger in baseball history, regardless of league or position. The legends about this tragic figure, cut down by a brain tumor at age 36, are as numerous as his homers. Contemporary experts agree—Gibson was special. Walter Johnson saw him play and said, "He can do everything," and said Gibson was better than Bill Dickey. Branch Rickey said that as good as his own **ROY CAMPANELLA** was, "Josh could do better." Gibson was the second player elected by the Negro Leagues Committee, after Satchel Paige.

ABOVE AND RIGHT:
Roy Campanella wore these shin guards in the 1950s. The use of high-impact plastics was not as much a part of the gear in those days.
OPPOSITE: *Josh Gibson was truly an impressive batter and catcher.*

Speaking of Campy, he too was a Negro Leagues star, while also playing in the Mexican League. It was his good fortune to be still young enough when the Dodgers and Jackie Robinson broke the "color barrier." Campy joined the majors in 1948 and proceeded to win three NL MVP awards and help Brooklyn win five NL pennants and the 1955 World Series. In early 1958, Campanella was seriously injured in a car accident. He became a near quadriplegic, but so beloved was he by baseball and fans that a then-record 93,000 people showed up in Los Angeles at a fundraising exhibition game. He remained a big part of baseball and the Dodgers until his death in 1993.

A PAIR OF YANKEES

As good as the Yankees were from the 1930s–'60s, they could have afforded to have their catcher focus on defense and handling pitchers. The Bombers had offense to spare. However, they were blessed with two Hall of Famers in that era who combined outstanding offense with terrific work behind the plate. **BILL DICKEY** was the first catcher to wear No. 8 for the Yanks, from 1928 to 1943 and again in 1946. In a lineup that in the beginning included Babe Ruth and Lou Gehrig, then Gehrig and Joe DiMaggio, Dickey more than held his own, batting above .300 in eleven seasons.

As with catchers then and now, Dickey was a leader on the field, inspiring the Yankees more with quiet hard work than with rah-rah style.

Just four years later, another superstar settled into place at Yankee Stadium. **YOGI BERRA** took Dickey's spot (and his No. 8 jersey) and ran with it, though not very fast. However, Berra did win three AL MVP awards, had five seasons with 100-plus RBI, and helped the Yanks win 10 World Series (and 14 AL pennants). He holds several offensive Series records, including hits and games.

ABOVE: Bill Dickey not only contributed mightily at the plate, he called games for Hall of Famers like Waite Hoyt and Red Ruffing.

He Said It

YOGI BERRA (above) deserves his place as a baseball immortal for his sterling work on the field and at the plate. However, he holds a beloved place in a wider American culture thanks to his somewhat flexible relationship with the English language. Here, from the book called *I Didn't Say Some of the Things I Said*, are some of his more famous unexpected aphorisms:

> "When you come to a fork in the road . . . take it!"
> "I usually take a two-hour nap from one to four."
> "You can observe a lot by watching."
> "It gets late early out here."
> "If the world were perfect, it wouldn't be."
> "It ain't over 'til it's over."

MODERN MASTERS

A pair of slugging catchers followed in the footsteps of Johnny Bench (see next page) with their offensive fireworks and solid defensive work. **GARY CARTER** became the Expos regular catcher in 1977 and also established his offensive credentials that year with 31 homers—one of nine seasons with 20-plus dingers. "The Kid," as he was sometimes known, was well-liked for his bright smile and friendly attitude. He was an 11-time All-Star; in fact, he won two All-Star Game MVPs and was often among the leaders in the fan voting. His defense improved tremendously the more he played; he would lead the NL in most catching categories at one time or another.

Another great catcher of this era didn't land in the majors to stay until he was 23, but he stuck around for a 23-season stretch. **CARLTON FISK** retains a permanent place in baseball history for his 1975 World Series Game Six-winning homer, which he famously "waved fair" in Fenway Park. However, that was just one moment in a long career that started as the 1972 AL Rookie of the Year. Fisk played for Boston until 1980, when he signed with the White Sox (famously reversing his No. 27 to become No. 72 in Chicago). He had been great with Boston, and he was good in Chicago, setting career highs in 1985 with 37 homers and 107 RBI. Solid and unyielding, Fisk was a great example of the toughness needed to excel at this difficult position.

TED SIMMONS

A catcher who can hit is one of baseball's rarest commodities. The Cardinals found one in the first round of the 1967 draft. After Simmons took over as the starter in 1971, he played 150 or more games seven times with six .300-plus seasons during that span. Durable and dependable, nothing better in a catcher. He had 193 hits in 1975, giving him the record for catchers with 150 games or more. He is second all-time among catchers in RBI and hits.

Carlton Fisk NIGHT

27

72

Tuesday, June 22, 1993
Comiskey Park

MIKE PIAZZA

Sometimes No. 62 can be No. 1. Piazza was famously taken by the Dodgers in the 62nd round of the MLB Draft in 1988. Today's amateur draft ends after 40 rounds! Part of the reason Piazza was picked was his godfather, LA manager Tommy Lasorda. But his bat soon showed that he was more than a charity pick and he was the 1993 NL Rookie of the Year. Few catchers in history slugged as well as Piazza. His 396 homers as a backstop (out of 427 overall) are the most all time. He also hit for average, with a career .308 mark. At first criticized for his defense, he vastly improved as his career went on, especially after moving to the Mets in 1998. The 12-time All-Star helped the Mets reach the 2000 World Series.

IVÁN RODRÍGUEZ

I-Rod was so good on defense they should retire the Gold Glove for the position. He won an all-time best 13 at baseball's toughest position. He also earned a catcher's-best 14 All-Star Game selections. Blessed with quick feet and a rocket arm, he was the quintessential field general behind the plate. You want hitting, too? He has 11 seasons with an average of .298 or better, including his AL MVP season of 1999 when he hit .332. Between long stints with the Rangers and Tigers, he enjoyed a career highlight in his single Florida Marlins season. The veteran catcher helped guide a team of young stars to the 2003 World Series title.

OPPOSITE (CLOCKEWISE FROM TOP LEFT): *A very young Gary Carter embarking on a Hall of Fame career behind the plate. Mike Piazza. Ted Simmons. Iván Rodríguez.*
TOP: *Here's a souvenir card from Carlton Fisk's special evening held by the White Sox on his retirement.*

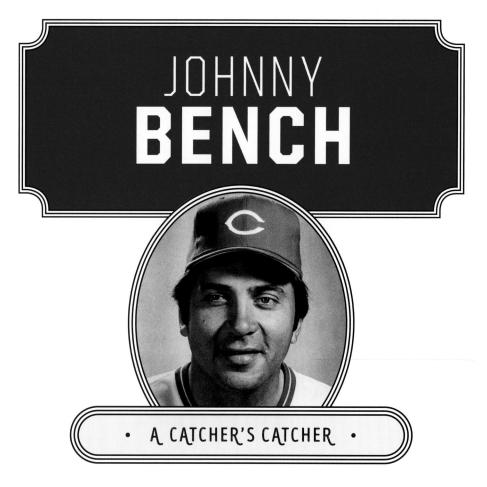

JOHNNY BENCH

• A CATCHER'S CATCHER •

When Major League Baseball put together its All-Time Team in 1999, the position that probably got the least debate was catcher. Johnny Bench was a shoo-in for a spot, joined by Yogi Berra. Bench was not only a 14-time All-Star and a two-time MVP, he also won 10 Gold Gloves and literally changed the way that catchers do their jobs. Johnny Bench was the modern exemplar of the catcher as all-around star.

Bench grew up in Oklahoma and had pro baseball on his mind from a young age. A second-round pick in the new amateur draft in 1965, Bench was Rookie of the Year in 1968. That season, he also won the first of his Gold Gloves, a rarity for a first-year player. His ability to catch one-handed using the then-new hinged mitt gave him the chance to show off his cannon arm to best effect. Bench led the way from pillow-pad catchers' mitts to the easy-to-handle models used today. He also was the first catcher to wear a helmet along with his mask.

At the plate, Bench was, if possible, even more effective. By his third full season, he was one of the best sluggers in the league, leading the NL with 45 homers and 148 RBI. He repeated that feat in 1972, but the best was yet to come. As a key cog in the Big Red Machine, Bench helped Cincinnati win World Series in 1975 and 1976, in the latter of which he was named MVP.

When he retired, he had hit more homers than any other catcher (Carlton Fisk and Mike Piazza have topped him since) and had more Gold Gloves (Iván Rodríguez now has 13). But no catcher before or since has combined the defensive excellence and offensive firepower of this young man from Oklahoma. How good was he? When he was elected to the Hall of Fame in 1989, he received the third-highest percentage of the vote to that time, trailing a couple of fellows named Aaron and Cobb.

CAREER STATS:	
YEARS:	17
HR:	389
RBI:	1,376
AVG:	.267

OPPOSITE: Johnny Bench's powerful right-handed swing made him a feared slugger, but what he loved most was driving in runs to help his teams win.

3

THE INFIELDERS

People say (and a famous movie expounded further) that baseball is a simple game. You throw the ball, you catch the ball. But on a Major League infield, that simplicity morphs into grace, athleticism, and a kind of geometric complexity. Infielders are challenged by hard ground balls, wicked line drives, sliding runners, dinky rollers, high choppers, and every manner of pop-up and bloop. The players must have lightning-quick reactions both of body and mind. With every pitch, the situation of the game changes and they must make new mental calculations in the split seconds before they have to make physical reactions. And those calculations can mean the difference between a win and a loss.

Was the ball hit hard enough to turn two? Can I cut down the guy at second on the bunt? Barehanded or glove on this roller? Dive or keep moving left? How fast is the batter or the runner? All those sorts of questions can be asked in the mind of a fielder as the ball leaves the bat and they must be answered before the ball reaches the fielder . . . in the blink of an eye. On the infield, the game is played in split seconds and with the angles and changes of direction of a pinball machine.

Each of the four infield positions comes with its own unique challenges, whether that means covering a base, going into the hole, holding on runners, or turning two with the grace of a dancer and the bravery of a bullfighter. But all four positions share the common bond of making the simple fielding of a grounder—catch the ball, throw the ball—into something a little like poetry. Which is itself, of course, often a mix of the simple and the sublime.

OPPOSITE: Jackie Robinson protects his base.

FIRST BASE

CAP ANSON

Baseball's first great hitting star flourished in the early days of the National League, becoming the first player to reach 3,000 hits in a career (if you count his five National Assocation years). Adrian "Cap" Anson was the leader of the Chicago NL team, acting as star, captain (hence the nickname), and finally manager. With .300-plus averages in 24 of his 27 seasons, his skills at the plate were the finest of the first quarter-century of the pro game. Anson was also a manager for 20 years and was one of the sport's first true nationally known stars.

DAN BROUTHERS

"Big Dan" was Babe Ruth before Ruth was born. He led the NL in slugging average from 1881 through 1886 and also led in homers twice. Sure, his single-season high was 14, but through 1888 he had hit enough to be the league's career leader. It was a different game, and no one swatted the ball back then like Big Dan.

OPPOSITE: Cap Anson was an integral part of the Chicago NL club from 1876–'97.
ABOVE: This hand-colored photocard shows Dan Brouthers in the uniform of the Detroit Wolverines.
LEFT: Jeff Bagwell

JEFF BAGWELL

That wide stance. Those massive legs. That power bat. And he could steal bases, too? Bagwell was part of Houston's "Killer Bs" lineup for 15 seasons, regularly crushing tape-measure homers—he had a career total of 449. Bagwell also made Astro fans—and fantasy baseball players—swoon by stealing double-digit bases 10 times, with a career high of 31, a rarity for first sackers. He was the 1991 NL Rookie of the Year and the 1994 NL MVP. He topped 30 homers, 100 RBI, and 100 runs each season from 1996 through 2001, a rare feat matched by only five others. He's the Astros career leader in homers and ribbies, too.

ORLANDO CEPEDA

Cepeda followed Roberto Clemente as one of the first stars to emerge from Latin America. The native of Puerto Rico joined the Giants in 1958 and quickly earned the love of the team's new fans in San Francisco by winning NL Rookie of the Year honors. He led the NL in homers and RBI in 1961, and was part of the Giants' 1962 pennant-winning team. Cepeda was traded to St. Louis in 1966, and in his first full season with the team, he led the Cardinals to a World Series title and was named NL MVP.

JIMMIE FOXX

The man known in his time as "The Beast" doesn't often get the notice of many when the topic is great all-time sluggers. But it wasn't until 1966 that he lost his spot behind Babe Ruth as baseball's number two homer hitter, and he hit more homers in the 1930s than anyone, including Gehrig, Simmons, DiMaggio, and other stars of the day. A three-time MVP, the 1933 Triple Crown winner, and a two-time World Series champ with the Athletics, Foxx deserves a permanent place at the slugger's head table.

TOP: *Shown here with the Braves, Orlando Cepeda (with mitt) had some of his best years with the Giants.*
RIGHT: *Few men were more fearsome at the plate than "Ol' Double X," Jimmie Foxx.*

WHO'S ON FIRST?

★ ★ ★

One of baseball's most famous "teams" is filled with some very curious names. They are recited by the great Abbott and Costello (below) performing their immortal "Who's on First?" routine. As we begin our visit with Hall of Fame fielders, here's the rundown of the nicknames with which manager Bud Abbott so baffles poor new catcher Lou Costello.

1B	Who	CF	Because
2B	What	RF	(not mentioned)
3B	I Don't Know	P	Tomorrow
SS	I Don't Give a Darn	C	Today
LF	Why		

HANK GREENBERG

Some might look at Hank Greenberg's career and wonder what might have been, had he not spent four-plus prime seasons serving his country during World War II. Greenberg, of course, never thought that, and had no problem with being one of the first to join the war. In fact, he signed up months before Pearl Harbor. He sandwiched his service with some serious slugging: three home run crowns (including 58 in 1938), two MVPs, and a World Series ring before, and another homer title and a world championship after. Wonder not at what might have been, marvel instead at what was. Greenberg also deserves praise for the way he handled his status as perhaps the first nationally famous Jewish ballplayer. In 1934, he chose not to play on Yom Kippur. Though at the time it was barely noted, over time it became another symbol of his character.

HARMON KILLEBREW

Just look at him. He just looks like a home-run hitter. Broad shoulders, strong chest, big arms to swing for the fences . . . which he did with regularity, leading the AL in homers six times while with the Senators/Twins franchise. Highlights included the Twins' 1965 AL pennant and then his own 1969 MVP award. But for all his fierce hitting and a nickname like "Killer," few baseball men were as gentle or beloved as this towering Twin.

*OPPOSITE: **Harmon Killebrew played some serious third base early in his career.***
*BELOW: **Hank Greenberg***

BUCK LEONARD

Along with his prodigious batting talents—a Negro National League batting and home-run champ—Leonard was a leader. On a Homestead Grays team that included stars such as Josh Gibson and that won nine NNL titles, Leonard was the captain and cleanup hitter.

WILLIE MCCOVEY

Ruth had Gehrig, Mays had McCovey. "Stretch" teamed with the "Say-Hey Kid" to lead the Giants throughout the 1960s, whacking 650 homers between them. In Mays's shadow, McCovey's accomplishments are sometimes dimmed, but they deserve the full light of day. His rate of a homer every 15.7 at-bats topped such stars as Gehrig, Aaron, and, yes, Mays. He remains fourth all-time with 18 grand slams. He led the NL in homers three times and was the 1969 MVP. "Willie Mac" more than deserved the honor given him in 2000 with the naming of McCovey Cove outside the Giants' new waterfront ballpark in San Francisco.

EDDIE MURRAY

Teddy Roosevelt would have loved Eddie Murray. Few players walked more silently through the game, and few carried a bigger or more versatile stick. Among switch-hitters, Murray is second only to Mickey Mantle in homers and to Pete Rose in hits. He's also one of only six players with 500 homers and 3,000 hits. Murray played more than 3,000 games with five clubs, though his greatest years were in Baltimore, where he was Rookie of the Year and a seven-time All-Star. He also had more RBI than any other player in the 1980s, though in typical fashion, he led the league only once and that in strike-shortened 1981. He also came through in the clutch, ranking third all-time with 19 grand slams. Quiet but steady and deadly, that was Murray.

TOP: ***Buck Leonard***
LEFT: ***Long and lean at 6'4", Willie McCovey***
had a smooth home-run swing
OPPOSITE: ***Eddie Murray***

The Infielders

GEORGE SISLER

A fine-fielding first baseman, Sisler was an all-around terrific hitter. The Browns' star led the AL at least once in nine key offensive stats. He twice batted better than .400 and was a four-time stolen base champ. He also held the single-season record—during one of six seasons with 200 or more hits—with 257 hits. (Ichiro Suzuki broke that mark in 2004 with 262.) Sisler's .340 career mark included seven seasons above that average with a career high of .420 in 1922.

TOP AND LEFT: George Sisler battled vision problems in the latter part of his career, but remained a .300 hitter until his retirement in 1930.

WILLIE STARGELL

The man known as "Pops" was called that for his fatherly attitude and for his leadership of a young Pirates team in their 1979 World Series year. But he could just as easily have earned it for his power. A solid outfielder in the 1960s, he blossomed late (in fact, he didn't move to first base until 1975). His 48 homers in 1971 led the NL, and he helped the Pirates win the World Series that year. Eight years later, having moved to first base, he was the co-NL MVP with far less gaudy numbers. Instead, it was his inspiring leadership and cheerleading that, combined with 32 timely homers, made him a winner again.

BILL TERRY

Just ahead of Sisler on the career hitting chart was his contemporary Bill Terry. The Giants' first baseman was to NL pitchers what Sisler was to those in the AL: a feared hitting machine. He had nine straight seasons of .320 or better with a career best .401 in 1930. He helped the Giants win three NL pennants and the 1933 World Series, the latter after having taken over as the Giants manager from the great John McGraw. He led them to two more pennants before retiring.

BELOW LEFT: Bill Terry covers his base.
BELOW: Willie Stargell was a powerful slugger and a dynamic leader.

LEFT: *Frank Thomas*
OPPOSITE: *Jim Thome*

FRANK THOMAS

Frank Thomas earned the nickname of "The Big Hurt" for what he did to baseballs. He was one of the most-feared sluggers of the 1990s, with seven 30-homer seasons in the decade (and he's a member of the exclusive 500-homer club at 521). Thomas was more than a slugger, though, leading the league in walks and on-base percentage four times, and was the 1997 AL batting champ. Thomas won back-to-back AL MVPs in 1993 and 1994. Moving to DH for most of the second part of his 19-year career, 16 of those seasons with the White Sox, his hitting credentials are more than Hall-worthy.

JIM THOME

This slugging lefty was one of those players who was never the No. 1 superstar but was always among the very best. His consistent power output helped make him a legend in Cleveland, which unveiled his statue in 2014. When you're in the conversation with names like Ruth, Aaron, and Mays—and Thome's 612 career homers puts him there—you're in good company. He had 12 30-homer seasons, including six with 40 or more, topped by a career-best 52 in 2002. He put in solid seasons at first base before enjoying life as a DH. Along with Cleveland, he spent time with the Phillies, White Sox, and three other clubs.

LOU GEHRIG

· THE IRON HORSE ·

In baseball's pantheon, Lou Gehrig plays the role of the tragic hero. Perhaps no other player is as well known for what he said while he was dying as for what he did while he was playing. But Gehrig's July 4, 1939, speech (delivered shortly after he'd received a diagnosis of the disease, amyotrophic lateral sclerosis, or ALS, that would take his life just two years later) remains one of baseball's—one of America's—most poignant moments of both courage and heartbreak.

Gehrig grew up in New York City, the son of German immigrants. He clung to his parents like glue for most of his life; they watched closely as he grew into a star athlete. By the time he was in high school, he was inviting comparisons to Babe Ruth. At 22, he was the Yankees' starting first baseman. Over the next 14 seasons, Gehrig put up incredible numbers. On a team that had

CAREER STATS:	
YEARS:	17
AVG:	340
HR:	493
RBI:	1,995
HITS:	2,721

Ruth hitting ahead of him, he still led the AL in RBI five times, including a still-record 184 in 1931. He won the 1934 Triple Crown, partly with a .363 average that was fourth-best of his career. He didn't score fewer than 125 runs in any season from 1926 through 1937.

As with any player, and perhaps more than most, the numbers don't tell the whole story. Gehrig was loyal to his managers and family, he was shy and reserved around women (until he met his beloved wife Eleanor), and, of course, he was dedicated to his craft. His consecutive-game streak of 2,130 games, though since bested by Cal Ripken Jr., in 1995, remains his most honored mark.

The death of "the Iron Horse" in 1941 shattered baseball. His legacy, however, lives on thanks to his deeds . . . and his words. "Today," said the dying man, "I consider myself the luckiest man on the face of the earth."

OPPOSITE: *Lou Gehrig's slugging helped the Yankees win six World Series while he was with the team from 1923 to 1939.*

ABOVE: *Lou Gehrig strikes a pensive pose.*

CERTIFICATE

Souvenir for a slugger: Lou Gehrig received this document for one of his many career milestones. The signatures are of Joe Cronin and Warren Giles, both of whom would later join Gehrig in the Hall of Fame.

200 HOME RUN CLUB

THE AMERICAN AND NATIONAL LEAGUES OF PROFESSIONAL BASEBALL

certify that _Lou Gehrig_

of _The New York Yankees_

hit the 200th Home Run of his Major League Career

at _Sportsman's Park, St. Louis_

on _June 20, 1931_ to become

the _Fifth_ player in history to achieve this distinction.

Joseph E. Cronin
PRESIDENT, THE AMERICAN LEAGUE

Warren Giles
PRESIDENT, THE NATIONAL LEAGUE

PLAYER'S CONTRACT

Lou Gehrig's 1926 contract with the Yankees. Note that salary and the loyalty clause!

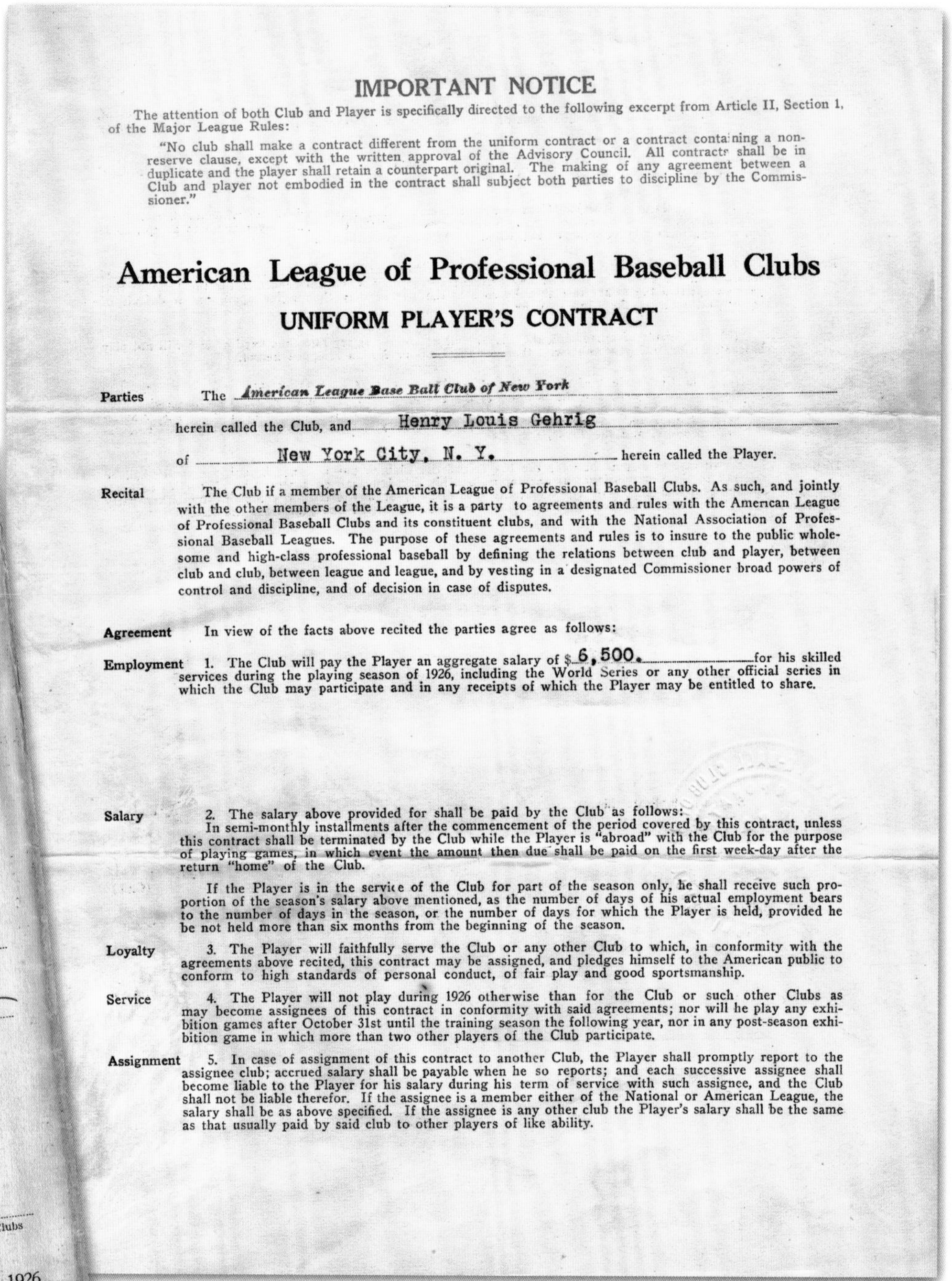

IMPORTANT NOTICE

The attention of both Club and Player is specifically directed to the following excerpt from Article II, Section 1, of the Major League Rules:

"No club shall make a contract different from the uniform contract or a contract containing a non-reserve clause, except with the written approval of the Advisory Council. All contracts shall be in duplicate and the player shall retain a counterpart original. The making of any agreement between a Club and player not embodied in the contract shall subject both parties to discipline by the Commissioner."

American League of Professional Baseball Clubs

UNIFORM PLAYER'S CONTRACT

Parties — The American League Base Ball Club of New York herein called the Club, and Henry Louis Gehrig of New York City, N. Y. herein called the Player.

Recital — The Club if a member of the American League of Professional Baseball Clubs. As such, and jointly with the other members of the League, it is a party to agreements and rules with the American League of Professional Baseball Clubs and its constituent clubs, and with the National Association of Professional Baseball Leagues. The purpose of these agreements and rules is to insure to the public wholesome and high-class professional baseball by defining the relations between club and player, between club and club, between league and league, and by vesting in a designated Commissioner broad powers of control and discipline, and of decision in case of disputes.

Agreement — In view of the facts above recited the parties agree as follows:

Employment — 1. The Club will pay the Player an aggregate salary of $ 6,500. for his skilled services during the playing season of 1926, including the World Series or any other official series in which the Club may participate and in any receipts of which the Player may be entitled to share.

Salary — 2. The salary above provided for shall be paid by the Club as follows:
In semi-monthly installments after the commencement of the period covered by this contract, unless this contract shall be terminated by the Club while the Player is "abroad" with the Club for the purpose of playing games, in which event the amount then due shall be paid on the first week-day after the return "home" of the Club.

If the Player is in the service of the Club for part of the season only, he shall receive such proportion of the season's salary above mentioned, as the number of days of his actual employment bears to the number of days in the season, or the number of days for which the Player is held, provided he be not held more than six months from the beginning of the season.

Loyalty — 3. The Player will faithfully serve the Club or any other Club to which, in conformity with the agreements above recited, this contract may be assigned, and pledges himself to the American public to conform to high standards of personal conduct, of fair play and good sportsmanship.

Service — 4. The Player will not play during 1926 otherwise than for the Club or such other Clubs as may become assignees of this contract in conformity with said agreements; nor will he play any exhibition games after October 31st until the training season the following year, nor in any post-season exhibition game in which more than two other players of the Club participate.

Assignment — 5. In case of assignment of this contract to another Club, the Player shall promptly report to the assignee club; accrued salary shall be payable when he so reports; and each successive assignee shall become liable to the Player for his salary during his term of service with such assignee, and the Club shall not be liable therefor. If the assignee is a member either of the National or American League, the salary shall be as above specified. If the assignee is any other club the Player's salary shall be the same as that usually paid by said club to other players of like ability.

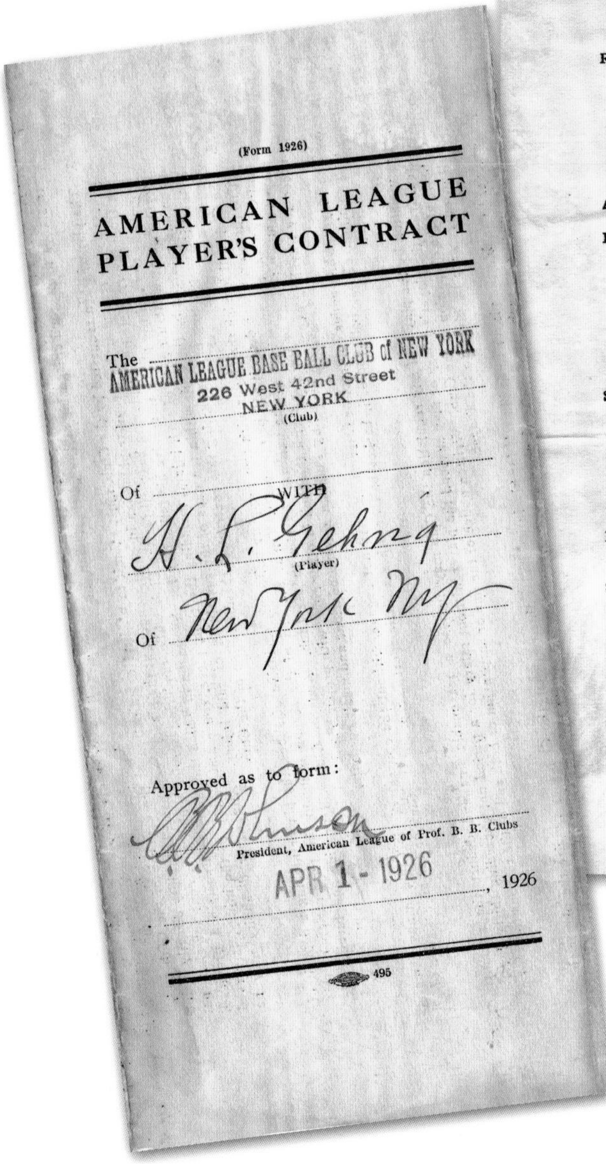

(Form 1926)

AMERICAN LEAGUE PLAYER'S CONTRACT

The AMERICAN LEAGUE BASE BALL CLUB of NEW YORK
226 West 42nd Street
NEW YORK
(Club)

Of WITH

H. L. Gehrig
(Player)

Of New York NY

Approved as to form:

[signature]
President, American League of Prof. B. B. Clubs

APR 1 - 1926, 1926

495

Discipline   6. (a) The Player accepts as part of this contract the Regulations printed on the third page hereof, and also such reasonable modifications of them and such other reasonable regulations as the Club may announce from time to time.

(b) This contract may be terminated at any time by the Club or by any assignee upon ten days' written notice to the Player.

(c) The Major and Major-Minor League agreements and rules, and all amendments thereto hereafter adopted, are hereby made a part of this contract, and the Club and Player agree to accept, abide by, and perform all decisions of the Commissioner pursuant thereto.

Renewal   7 (a) On or before February 15th, 1927, by written notice to the Player at his last address of record with the Club, the Club or any assignee hereof may renew this contract for the term of that year except that the salary rate shlal be such as the parties may then agree upon, or, in default of agreement, such as the Club may fix.

(b) In default of agreement, the Player will accept the salary rate thus fixed or else will not play baseball during said year otherwise than for the Club or for an assignee hereof.

(c) The Club's right of reservation of the Player and of renewal of this contract as aforesaid for the succeeding year, and the promise of the Player not to play during said year otherwise than with the Club or an assignee hereof, have been taken into consideration in determining the salary specified herein and the undertaking by the Club to pay said salary is the consideration for both said reservation and promise, and the Player's service.

Disputes   8. In case of dispute between the Player and the Club or any assignee hereof, the same shall be referred to the Commissioner as an umpire, and his decision shall be accepted by all parties as final; and the Club and the Player agree that any such dispute, or any claim or complaint by either party against the other, shall be presented to the Commissioner within one year from the date it arose.

Special Covenants
See "Important Notice" above.

30" day of *March* A. D. 1926.

American League Base Ball Club of New York
(Club)

By *Jacob Ruppert* President

Henry Louis Gehrig
(Player)

REGULATIONS

1. The Playing Season for each year covered by this contract and all renewals hereof shall be as fixed by the American League of Professional Baseball Clubs, or, if this contract shall be assigned to a club in another league, then by the league of which such assignee is a member.

2. The player must keep himself in first-class physical condition and must at all times conform his personal conduct to standards of good citizenship and good sportsmanship.

3. The player, when requested by the Club, must submit to medical examination at the expense of the Club and, if necessary, to treatment by a regular physician in good standing at the player's expense. Disability directly resulting from injury sustained in playing baseball for the Club while rendering service under this contract shall not impair the right of the player to receive his full salary for the season in which the injury was sustained, provided, however, that written notice of such injury, including the time, place, cause and nature of the injury, is served upon and received by the Club within ten days of the sustaining of said injury. Any other disability may be ground for suspending or terminating this contract at the discretion of the Club.

4. The Club will furnish the player with two complete uniforms, exclusive of shoes, the player making a deposit of $30.00 therefor, which deposit will be returned to him at the end of the season or upon the termination of this contract, upon the surrender of the uniforms by him to the Club. And the Club will provide and furnish the player while "abroad" or traveling with the Club in other cities with proper board, lodging, and pay all proper and necessary traveling expenses, including Pullman accommodations and meals en route.

5. The Player, while under contract or reservation, shall not engage, without the consent of his Club, in any game or exhibition of baseball, football, basket ball or other athletic sport except for the Club or for an assignee of this contract.

6. For violation by the player of any regulation the Club may impose a reasonable fine and deduct the amount thereof from the player's salary or may suspend the player without salary for a period not exceeding thirty days, or both, at the discretion of the Club. Written notice of the fine or suspension or both and of the reasons therefor shall in every case be given to the Player.

7. In order to enable the player to fit himself for his duties under this contract, the Club may require the player to report for practice at such places as the Club may designate and to participate in such exhibition contests as may be arranged by the Club for a period of *Forty-five* days prior to the playing season without any other compensation than that herein provided, the Club, however, to pay the traveling expenses, including Pullman accomodations, and meals en route of the player from his home city to the training place of the Club, whether he be ordered to go there direct or by way of the home city of the club. In the event of the failure of the player to report for practice or to participate in the exhibition games, as provided for, a penalty by way of fine may be imposed by the Club, the same to be deducted from the compensation stipulated herein.

SECOND BASE

ROBERTO ALOMAR

Alomar was the best second baseman of the 1990s, earning 12 straight All-Star selections and 10 Gold Gloves. A career .300 hitter, Alomar was the leader of a Toronto team that won back-to-back World Series in 1992 and 1993. He began his career with San Diego, but had his greatest success up north and in Cleveland, where he had some of his most successful offensive seasons. Alomar's dad, Sandy, also played big-league ball, and Roberto got to play in Cleveland with his brother, catcher Sandy Jr.

CRAIG BIGGIO

Another Astros "Killer B," Biggio was one of the best-hitting second sackers of his generation. There have been a lot of right-handed sluggers in baseball history, but Biggio tops them all with his 668 career doubles. He also had speed, stealing 414 bags. Hits? He's in the 3,000-hit club. In fact, Biggio is the only player in baseball history with 3,000 hits, 600 doubles, 250 homers, and 400 steals. He was versatile on the field, too, starting his career as a catcher before earning four Gold Gloves at second. He also played centerfield for the Astros! Let us also honor his place in baseball trivia history: No batter in the modern era was hit by more pitches than Biggio, 285 plunks in 20 seasons.

ROD CAREW

From down Panama way came one of the finest pure hitters ever. Rod Carew could hit just about anything that came his way, winning seven AL batting titles with the Twins before moving to the Angels, for whom he collected his 3,000th career hit in 1985. His .388 in 1977 was the highest average since Ted Williams's .406 in 1941. Starting in 1967, when he was named AL Rookie of the Year, Carew was an All-Star for 18 consecutive seasons through 1984.

OPPOSITE: Roberto Alomar turns a double play.
TOP: Craig Biggio
RIGHT: Rod Carew perfected a flat, line drive–creating swing.

EDDIE COLLINS

Timing is everything. Eddie Collins had 14 seasons batting .325 or better, yet never won a batting title—those went to the great Ty Cobb. Collins did lead the AL in steals four times. One of the best all-around second basemen ever, Collins can also proudly point to the four World Series he won (three with the Athletics, one with the White Sox).

BOBBY DOERR

Doerr was a pro's pro, doing all the little things right and playing his role perfectly. On an offensive powerhouse like the Ted Williams–led Red Sox of the 1940s and 1950s, Doerr was a nine-time All-Star in recognition of his solid defense and table-setting abilities.

ABOVE: Bobby Doerr goes up and over a sliding White Sox player in double-play action.
LEFT: Eddie Collins

FRANKIE FRISCH

Frisch picked up the mantle of Christy Mathewson as a college man made good in the rough-and-tumble Major Leagues. "The Fordham Flash" was a multisport star in college and joined the Giants in 1919. He helped them win four pennants and two World Series with sterling defense and speed. He feuded with manager John McGraw eventually and was traded to St. Louis for 1927 for what proved a brilliant first season, as he set NL records for chances and putouts while batting .337. In 1928, he helped them win the first of four pennants; they captured world titles in 1931 and 1934. Frisch was the player-manager for the latter of those, leading the famous "Gas House Gang" to victory.

CHARLIE GEHRINGER

It's a good thing people were around to watch Charlie Gehringer put together a .320 career average and lead the AL in fielding seven times. Otherwise, you wouldn't have heard about it from him. Known as "The Mechanical Man" for his stolid, businesslike approach to the game, Gehringer let his play do all his talking. Gehringer's best season was 1937, in which he hit a career-high .371 and was named the AL MVP.

ABOVE: Charlie Gehringer shows the form that made him a .320 career hitter.
BELOW: Frankie Frisch makes the catch.

BELOW: *Napoleon Lajoie*
BELOW (RIGHT): *Bill Mazeroski's eight Gold Gloves stand testament to his prowess.*

NAPOLEON LAJOIE

The 20th century started off with a bang for this slick-fielding second baseman. Lajoie's .426 mark in 1901 was never topped for the rest of the century and was the first of his five AL batting titles. He had joined the new league's Athletics after debuting with the Phillies in 1896. By the end of the AL's first decade, having moved to the Indians in 1902, he was one of, if not the best, overall hitters in the league. He became so well liked in Cleveland that when he was player-manager from 1905 to 1909, the team was known as the Naps.

BILL MAZEROSKI

1960 World Series. Bottom of the ninth. Score tied. The home fans praying for a miracle. They get one. Pittsburgh's Bill Mazeroski smacks a pitch from the Yankees Ralph Terry over the left-field wall and for the first and still only time in baseball history, a World Series is won with a Game Seven homer. However, Maz is also well remembered for outstanding defense. His eight Gold Gloves are testament to that, along with a reputation as the best double-play turner ever. Some, in fact, say that Maz's skills with the glove are the best of any player at any position. One monster hit and 17 years of near-perfection: a Hall of Fame combination.

INFIELD SLANG

★ ★ ★

As we read about men who patrolled the "keystone sack" (second base),
here's a look at some of the great baseball slang slung around the bases:

AROUND THE HORN	A play that goes third-to-second-to-first
BALTIMORE CHOP	A hit that bounces high in the air off the dirt in front of home plate
CANDY HOP	A ball hit with a nice, easy bounce right to a fielder
CUE BALL	A ball hit off the end of the bat
THE DISH	Home plate
HOT CORNER	Third base
NEIGHBORHOOD PLAY	Usually the first part of a double play, when a fielder doesn't tag the base but gets the out call from the ump
STONE HANDS	a bad fielder

JOE MORGAN

Go ahead, put up your left elbow and give it a flap. You know that's one of the first things you picture when you think of Cincinnati's two-time MVP. What many forget is that Morgan was a nine-year vet (with Houston) when he finally joined the Big Red Machine in 1972. He was the sparkplug of that Reds dynasty that won three NL pennants and two World Series (the Reds also won the 1970 NL title, and Morgan later appeared in a final Series in 1983 with the Phillies). Morgan's speed was just one of his offensive weapons. His 266 career homers were once a record for second basemen. Morgan was perfect at setting the table for the big RBI men behind him, leading the NL in walks and on-base percentage four times each. With the Reds, he had six straight seasons with 49 or more steals. He also won five Gold Gloves.

JACKIE ROBINSON

After Babe Ruth, Jackie Robinson is perhaps the most famous baseball player of all time, not just for what he did with his bat and glove, but what he did with his heart. Robinson, of course, was the first African American player in the 20th century, brought in by the Dodgers' Branch Rickey to break the color line. Robinson endured taunts, threats, and flying spikes to rise above the rancor and display a fortitude that has made him an American hero. As a ballplayer, he was almost his own equal as a man, winning the first Rookie of the Year award in 1947 and the 1949 NL MVP trophy, and helping the Dodgers win their only World Series in Brooklyn in 1955. But what Robinson's 10 years in the big leagues really won was an epochal change in the nation.

RYNE SANDBERG

The man the Bleacher Bums proudly called "Ryno" was the complete package: a nine-time Gold Glove winner at second, plus five seasons with more than 30 stolen bases. The 1984 NL MVP hit double-digits in errors in only five of his 16 seasons while topping 20 homers six times. He won seven Silver Slugger awards as the top-hitting second baseman in the NL. He remains beloved in the hearts of Cubs fans everywhere.

OPPOSITE: Jackie Robinson was such a great all-around athlete that he was the first UCLA student ever to earn letters in four sports—baseball, football, basketball, and track.
TOP: Ryne Sandberg was beloved by the Bleacher Bums in Wrigley Field for his defense and his clutch hitting.
ABOVE: On a powerhouse roster of top hitters and pitchers, Joe Morgan emerged as the team leader.

ROGERS HORNSBY

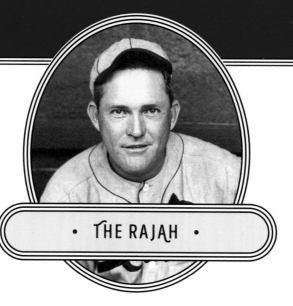

• THE RAJAH •

Talk about a hot streak: in the six seasons from 1920 through 1925, Rogers Hornsby averaged—averaged!—.397. He won six NL batting titles (he had a seventh in 1928), as well as slugging and on-base percentage titles. Among the highlights were a .424 average in 1924, 42 homers and 152 RBI in 1922, and a stunning 1.245 OPS in 1925. Those six seasons were a microcosm of the best career by a right-handed hitter in history. "The Rajah" had a career average of .358, second all-time behind Ty Cobb. He had nine slugging percentage titles, most ever in the NL. He topped 200 hits seven times. He won two Triple Crowns (1922 and 1925), a feat matched only by Ted Williams.

CAREER STATS:	
YEARS:	23
AVG:	.358
HR:	301
RBI:	1,584
HITS:	2,930

Hornsby was unmatched in talent on the field; his sole focus was hitting and winning, and pity the person who came between them and him. His versatility, leadership, and intelligence allowed him to manage five of the teams he also played for. In that role he was strict, tough, stubborn, and unyielding, but his legacy as a player is intact, and he enjoyed a rightful place on the All-Century Team at second base.

*RIGHT: **Rogers Hornsby starred in this book of advice for third basemen, though it was at second that he really made a name for himself.***

THIRD BASE

FRANK BAKER

If hitting two dingers in three days, albeit in the glare of the World Series, earns one the immortal nickname of "Home Run," what's left for later sluggers? But it was Frank Baker's fortune, and talent, to be a homer hitter in a time when they were rare birds indeed. With a 1910 World Series title already under his belt, Baker was part of the Athletics' $100,000 Infield of 1911, which returned to defend the team's crown. Facing the New York Giants, Baker hit a homer in Game Two and again in Game Three in crucial situations. A legend was born. In comparison to his contemporaries, Baker did excel at the long ball, leading the league four times, but his now-ironic nickname reflects a different time as much as it describes his skill.

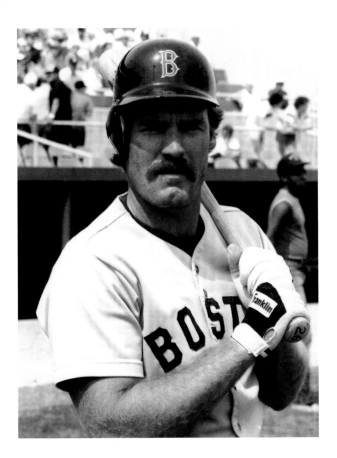

GEORGE BRETT

Brett was a complete hitter; he was not only the author of eleven .300-plus seasons, but was also often among league slugging leaders. His best season was 1980, when he posted a mark (.390) that remains the highest average in a full season—though he only played 117 games—since Ted Williams in 1941. He helped the Royals reach the 1980 World Series and turned them from a near joke into a regular contender. Brett had impressive longevity, too, as the only man to win batting titles in three decades: 1976, 1980, and 1990. He also was the first player to get 3,000 hits, 300 home runs, 600 doubles, 100 triples, 1,500 RBIs, and 200 stolen bases in a career. Brett was a solid fielder, a fiery leader, and an intense competitor (see the video of him reacting to being called out in the famous Pine-Tar Game in 1983).

WADE BOGGS

Chicken, anyone? Energized by his superstition-based pre-game meals, Boston's Wade Boggs put on a hitting clinic for most of the 1980s. Coming to the Red Sox at 23, he made a quick impact with a .349 average in 104 games in 1982. He became a regular atop the AL batting charts, with a career high of .368 in 1985 as part of a run of five batting titles in six seasons. Not known at first for his defense, he improved enough after moving to the Yankees in 1993 to win a pair of Gold Gloves. He also got a World Series ring in 1996. (Remember his triumphant ride around Yankee Stadium, riding double on the back of a police horse?) In a surprise for a player with only 118 career homers, he got his 3,000th career hit on a long ball while playing a swan-song season with the Tampa Bay Rays in 1999.

TOP: Wade Boggs's batting eye helped him lead the AL in on-base percentage six times.
RIGHT: George Brett was a lively presence on the Kansas City team.
OPPOSITE: Frank Baker had three seasons with 115 or more RBIs.

CHIPPER JONES

Jones made sure the Braves seasons didn't end after 162 games. His ball-crunching switch-hitting complemented the team's great pitching and led to 11 straight postseason trips in the 1990s and early 2000s. Destined for greatness as the number-one overall pick in 1990, from 1996 to 2003, he had consecutive 20-HR, 100-RBI seasons, highlighted by a career-high 45 bombs that helped him win the 1999 NL MVP. He played some outfield and shortstop, but mostly at third. In fact, his 1,623 RBI while manning the hot corner were tops for the position at his retirement.

RAY DANDRIDGE

They say that a great fielder can "pick it," and perhaps no one could pick it at third better than this Negro Leagues star. Dandridge played for the Detroit Stars, among other teams, and later spent several years in the Mexican League. He came tantalizingly close to the majors in the 1950s but was never given the chance to show off his talents there. How close did he come? He played in the Triple A American Association and batted .362 . . . at the age of 36.

JUDY JOHNSON

Win a few baseball trivia contests by knowing this Hall of Famer's real name: William. Whether by that name, his unusual nickname, or just by his reputation as one of the finest all-around players in the Negro Leagues, Johnson's is a name to know. He was the first third sacker chosen for the Hall from the Negro Leagues, thanks both to his long and storied career and to the great teams he helped, including the Homestead Grays and Pittsburgh Crawfords. Johnson was later a successful scout for several teams.

TOP LEFT: **Judy Johnson**
ABOVE: **Chipper Jones**
OPPOSITE: **Ray Dandridge excelled at third base no matter what country he played in.**

EDDIE MATHEWS

When Mike Schmidt was a kid aiming to become the best power-hitting third basemen ever, he was tracking the many accomplishments of Eddie Mathews. From 1952 through 1959—when Willie, Mickey, and the Duke were grabbing the headlines—no one hit more homers than Mathews. He ended up with 512 for his career, then the most by a third baseman. Never known for his glove work, he once said he was proudest of a defensive play he made to record the last out when his Milwaukee Braves won the 1957 World Series. Mathews is also the answer to this trivia question: What athlete was featured on the first issue of *Sports Illustrated* in 1954? He's also the only player to play with the Braves franchise in all three of its homes: Boston, Milwaukee, and Atlanta.

BROOKS ROBINSON

In 1964, he was named the AL MVP, then finished second in the 1966 voting to another Robinson, teammate Frank. That same duo combined to help the O's win the 1966 World Series, the 1969 AL pennant, and another Series in 1970. In that latter event, Robinson's defensive gems—including a diving stop of a Game One one-hop smash by Lee May—turned the tide and became part of Series lore. What's often forgotten is that his homer in that game provided the decisive run. In fact, Robinson hit .429 in that Series and was named the MVP. Solid if not spectacular with the bat, "the Human Vacuum Cleaner" was more than that with the glove. When you think great glovemen, Brooks Robinson and his third-base-record 16 Gold Gloves are at the top of the list.

TOP: *Eddie Mathews was the seventh player in history to reach 500 career homers.*
LEFT: *The Human Vacuum Cleaner, Brooks Robinson, lays out to snag another hard-hit ball.*

LEFT: *Ron Santo*
BELOW: *Deacon White*

RON SANTO

Cubs fans cheered when a veterans' committee welcomed Santo into the Hall in 2012. His gritty play on defense and a solid bat, along with a second career as a popular Cubs' TV and radio man, made him a legend in Wrigleyville. He was a key part of great Cubs teams that included fellow Hall members Ernie Banks, Fergie Jenkins, and Billy Williams, earning nine All-Star nods in the 1960s and early 1970s. Santo had eight 90-RBI seasons in a row and also won five Gold Gloves. During it all, he learned to cope with diabetes and later became an advocate for those with the disease.

DEACON WHITE

The Pre-Integration Committee assured White's entry into the Hall in 2013. Not bad for a player whose career ended in 1890. He was one of the most talented defenders in the gloveless era, fielding all positions, but mostly at third and catcher. He could hit too, leading his league in average twice and posting a career mark of .312. The Hall also provides this great bit of trivia on the talented White: His birth year of 1847 makes him the Hall of Fame player born the earliest!

MIKE SCHMIDT

• PHABULOUS IN PHILLY •

S tart any discussion of the best players ever at any position and settle in for a long talk. When you bring up third base, you're guaranteed to hear one name over and over: Michael Jack Schmidt of the Philadelphia Phillies.

Few players at any position combined outstanding hitting with top-notch defense as Schmidt did. He earned 10 straight Gold Gloves, handling Philly's artificial turf with ease. He also smashed 548 career homers, including a record eight NL homer titles. In fact, forget that he played third. His homer-hitting would put him amid the immortals at any position. He had 35 homers or more in 11 seasons, right up there near Babe and A-Rod. He

was one of only 15 players to hit four homers in a game, which he did against the Cubs at Wrigley Field in 1976. Toss in three NL MVP awards and helping the Phillies win their first-ever World Series in 1980, and you've got the complete package.

Schmidt looked like it came easy to him, but fans forget that he struggled at the plate early on, and that his home-run swing came only after some adjustments in his third season. In fact, he didn't win his first MVP award until he was 31. And this third basemen had to learn the position in the minors; believe it or not, Schmidt was a shortstop in high school and college.

CAREER STATS:	
YEARS:	18
AVG:	.267
HR:	548
RBI:	1,595
HITS:	2,234

OPPOSITE: Mike Schmidt posted career highs in homers (48) and RBI (121) while leading the Phillies to their first World Series in 1980.

SHORTSTOP

LUIS APARICIO

Many experts put Luis Aparicio just a hair behind Ozzie Smith on the list of best defensive shortstops. Add in Aparicio's nine straight AL stolen-base titles and you've got a very versatile star. The 1956 AL Rookie of the Year, he won nine Gold Gloves, the last in 1970 at the age of 36, and he helped the White Sox win the 1959 pennant and the Orioles to win the 1966 World Series. He was elected to the Hall of Fame in 1984, the first Venezuelan so honored.

ERNIE BANKS

"Let's play two!" Was there ever a player who simply loved the game more than Ernie Banks? The power-hitting shortstop (though he played first base the last ten years of his career) was blessed with wonderful talent at the plate in a career spent with the Chicago Cubs. Banks played 2,528 games but never appeared in a World Series. He was so good, however, that he won back-to-back MVPs (1958 and '59) on second-division clubs.

LUKE APPLING

Appling was not known for his fielding, but in an era when shortstops were more often known for their gloves, he stood out at the plate. In 1936, he became the first shortstop to lead the AL in batting, a feat he repeated in 1943. His bat kept him in the lineup often enough that when he retired in 1950, he held all career records for AL shortstops, including games played, assists, and putouts. Appling was also known for his endless discussions of his physical state, leading to the famous nickname, "Old Aches and Pains."

ABOVE LEFT: Luis Aparicio played 18 seasons with the White Sox, Orioles, and Red Sox, finishing his career in Boston in 1973.

ABOVE RIGHT: Luke Appling posted a career-best average of .388 in 1936.

OPPOSITE: Ernie Banks was as well known for his sunny personality as for his sweet home-run swing.

LOU BOUDREAU

Imagine if Marcus Semien, the 2019 All-MLB shortstop, not only played for Oakland, but was also its manager. Fans would be stunned at such a development, but for Lou Boudreau, it was no big deal. A three-time All-Star shortstop in his fifth season, Boudreau boldly asked to take over as the Indians' manager in 1942. To everyone's surprise, he was given the job and became, at 24, the youngest person to start a season as a manager. While continuing his fine play (including a 1944 AL batting title and a 1948 AL MVP award while batting .355), Boudreau became a creative manager. He invented the "Williams Shift," to counteract Ted Williams. He led Cleveland to the 1948 World Series championship. After retiring, he was a longtime broadcaster for the Cubs.

JOE CRONIN

Joe Cronin held just about every leadership position you can in baseball. After starting with the Pirates in 1926–27, he played a solid shortstop with the Washington Senators and was their player-manager by 1933, when he led them to their last AL pennant. Though he was married to the Senators' owner's niece/adopted daughter, he was traded after the 1934 season to the Red Sox, taking over as Boston's manager and shortstop. He took them to a pennant in 1946, though he had stopped playing regularly after the 1941 season. Cronin became the Sox GM, and in 1959 was made the president of the American League, a baseball man through and through.

DEREK JETER

To a long line of Yankee heroes and leaders, add this record-setting shortstop. Jeter was a 14-time All-Star, the 1996 Rookie of the Year, a two-time Hank Aaron Award winner, and a Roberto Clemente Award winner in 2009. Jeter was the heart and soul of Yankee teams that almost never missed the postseason. "The Captain" played in a remarkable 158 postseason games in 33 different series, posting a clutch .308 average. He was part of World Series winners in 1996, 1998, 1999, 2000, and 2009. He was the MVP of the 2000 Series when he hit .409 with a pair of homers. Jeter joined the 3,000-hit club in 2011 and made it memorable, smacking an opposite-field homer in front of the Yankee faithful. As of his retirement, he ended up sixth all-time in hits with 3,465. He capped off a remarkable Yankee Stadium career with a walk-off single in his final home at-bat.

TOP: Lou Boudreau would prove outstanding as both a player and manager.
MIDDLE: Boudreau used this glove during his Hall of Fame career.
LEFT: Joe Cronin's leadership talents were apparent on and off the field.
OPPOSITE: Derek Jeter

SENATE RESOLUTION

Making the Hall of Fame is call for honors galore; the Georgia State Senate bestowed this award on native son Luke Appling in 1964.

Georgia State Senate

A RESOLUTION

Congratulating Luke Appling on being voted into the Baseball Hall of Fame.

WHEREAS, Luke Appling was voted into the Baseball Hall of Fame on Monday, February 17, 1964; and

WHEREAS, this honor is so richly deserved and so long overdue; and

WHEREAS, he achieved the extraordinary lifetime batting average of 310 in twenty seasons with the Chicago White Sox, and played more games at shortstop than any other player in history; and

WHEREAS, "Ol' Aches and Pains", as he is known by baseball fans throughout the nation, is the second Georgian and the 101st player to receive this greatest of baseball honors;

NOW, THEREFORE, BE IT RESOLVED BY THE SENATE that Luke Appling is hereby congratulated on being elected to the Baseball Hall of Fame and for bringing honor and recognition to the State of Georgia;

BE IT FURTHER RESOLVED that the Secretary of the Senate is authorized and directed to send an appropriate copy of this resolution to Luke Appling and to the Baseball Hall of Fame.

Senate Resolution 220.   Adopted in Senate February 20, 1964.

By Senators Brown of the 34th, Brewer of the 39th, Wesberry of
        the 37th, MacIntyre of the 40th, Salome of the
        36th and Coggin of the 35th.

PRESIDENT OF THE SENATE   SECRETARY OF THE SENATE

BARRY LARKIN

In 1990, Larkin led the Reds to a World Series triumph over the Athletics, batting .353. In 1995, he stole a career-high 51 bags and his second of three Gold Gloves on his way to the NL MVP award. A year later, he was the first shortstop ever with a 30-30 season. Larkin combined his all-around baseball skills with great leadership on and off the field, earning the 1993 Roberto Clemente Award. In 19 seasons, all with the Reds, Larkin earned an honored spot in the long history of the ballclub.

POP LLOYD

The stories about Pop Lloyd are so amazing, you really wish that video was around when he played in the Negro Leagues in the 1920s and '30s. He was supposedly the finest fielding shortstop around, along with having a powerful batting stroke. The records suggest he never hit less than .362 in five Cuban league seasons, which was one of his many stops in a 20-plus-year career. Lloyd was known as the "Black Wagner," which the great Honus said he considered an honor.

PEE WEE REESE

Nicknamed Pee Wee as a child, Harold Reese grew up in Kentucky, but went on to earn a huge fan base in Brooklyn. The beloved shortstop's leadership and talent brought seven pennants and the 1955 World Series to the Dodgers faithful. His gentlemanly ways and talent on the field were a big hit with the long-suffering fans of "Da Bums." Reese was a 10-time All-Star and a solid, if unspectacular hitter. However, he made up for any lack of pop with an overdeveloped sense of leadership, a skill most in evidence in 1947, when he was one of several key players who helped smooth the transition of Jackie Robinson into baseball.

TOP LEFT: *Pop Lloyd's big hands earned him a nickname from his fans in the Cuban League: El Cuchara, or the Shovel.*

TOP RIGHT: *Barry Larkin*

ABOVE: *Pee Wee Reese goes through his paces to entertain newswire photographers.*

SCORESHEET

Notice the "2131" mark at the top of this scoresheet?
That could only mean that it came from Cal Ripken Jr.'s
record-setting game in 1995.

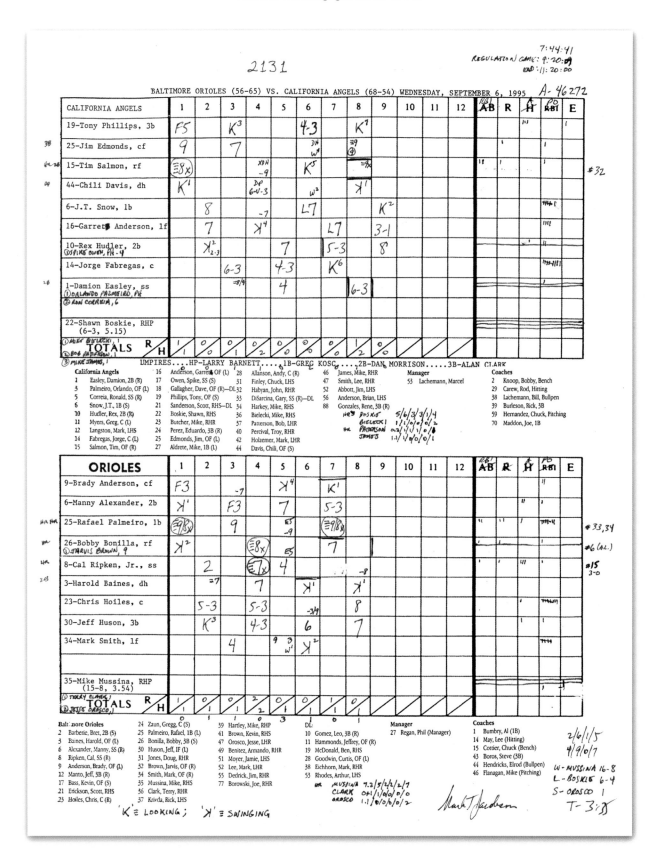

CAL RIPKEN JR.

If central casting had been in charge of finding the man to break Lou Gehrig's streak, they probably couldn't have done better than the guy who actually did it. Raised in a baseball family, Cal Ripken Jr. broke the mold for shortstops, the first tall, powerful man to play the position at Gold Glove level. A two-time MVP, he led the Orioles to the 1983 World Series title, but his defining trait was his perseverance. Ripken played 2,632 straight games, from 1982 to 1998. The night he broke Gehrig's mark of 2,130 was, for some, baseball's rebirth after the devastating 1994 strike. When baseball needed a hero, Ripken filled the role.

RIGHT: There were few on-field movements that escaped the awareness of Cal Ripken Jr.

IRON MEN

★ ★ ★

Cal Ripken Jr. is rightly honored for his consecutive-game streak, while Lou "the Iron Horse" Gehrig (see page 86) was the target Ripken aimed for. Here's a list, topped by those two, of the longest streaks in baseball history.

PLAYER	YEARS	GAMES
CAL RIPKEN, JR.	1982–1998	2,632
LOU GEHRIG	1925–1939	2,130
EVERETT SCOTT	1916–1925	1,307
STEVE GARVEY	1975–1983	1,207
MIGUEL TEJADA	2000–2007	1,152
BILLY WILLIAMS	1963–1970	1,117
JOE SEWELL	1922–1930	1,103
STAN MUSIAL	1952–1957	895
EDDIE YOST	1949–1955	829
GUS SUHR	1931–1937	822

PHIL RIZZUTO

Though most people remember The Scooter from his long tenure behind the mic for the Yankees, he was one of the key players on the Bronx Bombers' World Series run in the 1950s. He helped them win nine AL pennants and seven world championships. On a 1950 team that included Yogi Berra and Joe DiMaggio, it was Rizzuto who was named the AL MVP for his scrappy hitting and outstanding defense.

ALAN TRAMMELL

A six-time All-Star and four-time Gold Glove winner, Trammell was the glue that held the amazing 1984 Tigers together. They put together the best record in team history and powered to a World Series win in which, naturally, Trammell was the MVP after batting .450 with six RBI. Trammell helped pave the way for today's big-hitting shortstops. In 1987, he hit .343 and 28 homers and 105 RBI, the first shortstop to reach all those marks in a year. Trammell teamed with second baseman Lou Whitaker for 1,918 games, an all-time mark for a keystone-sack combo.

ARKY VAUGHAN

Joseph Floyd Vaughan grew up in California, but was born in Arkansas—hence the nickname. A nine-time All-Star, Vaughan led the NL at various times in triples, runs, walks, and slugging average, as well as batting average, on-base percentage, games, plate appearances, and stolen bases. He played in his only World Series in 1947, while finishing up his career with four seasons in Brooklyn.

OPPOSITE: *Holy Cow! It's Phil Rizzuto, a defensive leader of seven Yankees title winners.*
TOP: *Arky Vaughan*
RIGHT: *Alan Trammell*

HONUS WAGNER

What might a 2000s-era scouting report say about Honus Wagner? A five-tool player, he can do it all. Hit for average (eight NL batting titles, career .328); hit for power (six NL slugging average titles, led NL in doubles seven times); run (still 10th all-time with 723 steals); play defense (primarily a shortstop, he played all infield positions for the Pirates at one time or another); and throw ("His hands were so big, he sent handfuls of dirt to first base along with the ball."). Nearly a century after his last game in 1917, Wagner is still regarded as one of, if not the, best overall shortstops ever and one of the most dangerous and accomplished right-handed hitters.

JOHN MONTGOMERY WARD

Talk about a multitalented threat. "Monte" Ward began his career in 1878 primarily as a pitcher. In fact, in 1880 with Providence of the NL, he pitched the second-ever perfect game (just five days after the first: the third wouldn't come until 1904). Two years later, he pitched a record 18-inning shutout. An arm injury, however, pushed him to the outfield. No matter, he played center field and threw left-handed while his right recovered. By 1885, he was at shortstop and in 1887 batted a career-high .338. Amid all this, he managed to go to law school in the off-season, and it was under his legal leadership that the Players' League had its short run in 1890. He also managed in the League that same year, later leading the New York NL club to the 1894 league title. On and off the field, John Ward could do it all.

TOP: Honus Wagner
BOTTOM LEFT: John Montogomery Ward was an early proponent of ballplayers organizing to claim their rights.
BOTTOM RIGHT: Willie Wells
OPPOSITE: Robin Yount played his entire 20-year career with the Brewers, ending up with 3,142 hits.

WILLIE WELLS

Along with Pop Lloyd, Wells was one of the best shortstops of the Negro Leagues. Wells didn't boast Lloyd's batting prowess (though some sources give him a career mark above .330), but he was seriously slick on the field. His greatest talent might have been his arm, which was accurate with a lightning-quick release.

ROBIN YOUNT

Yount is one of only three players to win MVP awards at two different positions (the others are Stan Musial and Alex Rodriguez). Yount was a young shortstop when he was the 1982 MVP for Milwaukee, as they earned their first AL pennant. Seven years later, he was a centerfielder and an MVP, taking several more steps on the road to 3,000 hits and a rare spot in the Hall of Fame.

OZZIE SMITH

• THE WIZARD OF AAAHS! •

In the world that Ozzie Smith created over 19 big-league seasons, baseball was more than a simple game—it was art. Smith set a new and probably unapproachable standard for fielding excellence, not only by making all the routine plays so perfectly but by finding new ways almost every night to create one-of-a-kind highlights. In a very short time, he became the Wizard, whether of Oz or Aaahs!

Smith was good early. Though he stole 40 bases, he hit only .258, so you can point to his second-place finish in the 1978 Rookie of the Year balloting as an early indication that his defense was something special. In fact, he won the first of his shortstop-record 13 Gold Gloves in his third season with the San Diego Padres. Traded to St. Louis on December 10, 1981, he got off to a great start in his Cardinals career by earning his only World Series ring.

When he was in motion, fans truly couldn't look away: Diving this way and that, hopping up to throw to first—Smith caused many an opponent to toss his helmet in frustration after another onfield robbery.

He was never a tremendous hitter, reaching .300 only once in his career. Ozzie had tremendous speed, though, and stole 30 or more bases in 11 seasons. And once in a while, the magic in his hands stuck around when he came to the plate, never more so than in 1985. His Cardinals were tied with the Dodgers at two games apiece in the NL Championship Series. With one out in the bottom of the ninth, Smith hit the first left-handed home run of his switch-hitting career to win the game; St. Louis would go on to win the series in six games.

His trademark back flip to kick off and wrap up each season and each postseason series symbolized more than his joy at playing this kids' game. It symbolized just how Ozzie Smith had transformed this game, with glove and feet and hands, like a wizard.

CAREER STATS:	
YEARS:	19
AVG:	.262
SBs:	580
HITS:	2,460

OPPOSITE: *Ozzie Smith found much joy in the game.*

THE OUTFIELDERS

From the top of the upper deck, the outfield looks immense, sprawling. The eyes are drawn to the emerald, unworldly perfection of the grass, to the sharp red or brown outline of the warning track, and then, slowly, they refocus on the tiny white dots. Those dots are the outfielders. How can three little people cover so vast an area? From above, it looks impossible. You could put everyone from the bleachers in the outfield and still see yards and yards of green.

But somehow, those three players do just that. With speed, timing, technique, and practice, they can indeed cover that vast greensward. They don't catch everything, of course, but until you see them move, until you see them read the angle, cut down the ball, and fire it back in, you can't really understand why any ball hit out there doesn't give the hitter time to clear the bases. The geometry of moving ball and moving fielder is one of those many examples of baseball as poetry in motion.

That outfielders are such superb athletes is one reason, too, why many are known far and wide as the greatest offensive forces in the game's history. This chapter is dotted with players who earned their greatest fame not only in the pastoral pursuit of baseballs, but also in the earthier role of whacking them . . . far and wide.

OPPOSITE: Joe DiMaggio.

BABE RUTH

• THE GOLD STANDARD •

CAREER STATS:	
YEARS:	22
HR:	714
RBI:	2,214
AVG:	.342

For nearly his entire colorful, memorable, record-setting career, Babe Ruth so dominated baseball that decades later the sport is still feeling the effects. Today's home run heroes owe an ongoing debt of gratitude to the mighty Bambino. Few athletes in any sport can be said to have revolutionized their games as Ruth did by introducing sheer, raw power into baseball. With a sport reeling from the Black Sox scandal of 1919 and facing growing competition from other sports including boxing and college and pro football, baseball needed a savior. Following his move to the Yankees, Ruth stepped off the pitcher's mound (on which, by the way, he excelled—the only truly All-Star-caliber two-way player in the 20th century) and into the outfield to stay. From 1919 to 1931, he led the AL in slugging in all but one season, and in on-base percentage for nine of those years. In that time, he topped the league in homers every

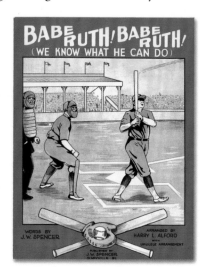

year but two. Consider the game saved.

That such a baseball talent appeared in the form of a life-loving man-child made his legend even greater. Ruth was a symbol of a high-living age, a rocket ride up the roller coaster that came down with a Depression crash. Writers of the time did their part to expand on the myth, but Ruth didn't do much to correct the record. ("Did you really call your shot in the 1932 World Series, Babe?" "Well, that's what it said in the papers, didn't it?") He played big, he lived large, he filled seats, he won games. No player since has combined all those things in ways equal to the Babe.

His 714 career homers, of course, were the standard of excellence until Hank Aaron came along, but even as Babe's place on the all-time list drops into bronze-medal territory, his legend remains. For all-around skills, for impact on the game, for combining personality and power, Babe Ruth remains baseball's gold standard.

OPPOSITE: During spring training, Babe Ruth used a hefty 54-ounce bat, his powerful wrists, his strong upper body, and his huge swing to generate enormous power.

CHRISTMAS CARD

Naturally, the umpire in this Christmas card from Babe Ruth, ca. 1930s, would have been "Red," not "Blue."

May this Greeting be the biggest hit I ever make
Babe Ruth

UNIFORM AGREEMENT

A Red Sox fan's least favorite document: This officially transferred Babe Ruth from Boston to the Yankees in 1919.

OPPOSITE: *The inimitable Babe "The Bambino" Ruth.*

LEFT FIELDERS

LOU BROCK

After being traded by the Cubs to the Cardinals in one of history's most lopsided deals, Brock used his speed to rewrite the record books, leading the NL in stolen bases eight times. His high-water mark was the 118 bases he swiped in 1974 to break Maury Wills's record. At his best in big games, Brock hit .394 in three World Series, two of which St. Louis won. When he retired in 1979, he was the all-time leader in steals with 938 (a mark later topped by Rickey Henderson).

JESSE BURKETT

Eighty-three years before Ron Blomberg became the first DH, Jesse Burkett was a DH in all but name. The man could flat-out hit, topping .400 twice and finishing his career in 1905 with a .342 lifetime average. His bunting skills were unmatched, and he could fly, stealing 25 or more bases nine times. He wasn't nearly as good in the outfield as he was at the plate, but his batting skills were certainly Hall of Fame caliber.

ED DELAHANTY

"Big Ed" was a lifetime .346 hitter, fifth all-time, including three seasons of .404 or better. Though he had a classic line drive swing perfectly made for the game at the time, he had some pop, too. In a game in 1896, Delahanty became only the second man with four homers in a game. In an era of great hitters, Delahanty stood out.

GOOSE GOSLIN

Leon "Goose" Goslin was a great teammate in more ways than one. Not only did he have a wonderful, almost childlike attitude toward the game ("It was more than fun," he once said. "It was heaven."), but he could drive his teammates home like few others. Goslin topped 100 RBI 12 times, among the most ever. He topped .315 seven times, while helping both the Senators and Tigers win World Series championships.

OPPOSITE: *Lou Brock is the only player in baseball history with 12 straight seasons with 50 or more stolen bases (1965–76).*
TOP LEFT: *Ed Delahanty was one of the great hitters of the 19th century.*
TOP RIGHT: *Jesse Burkett models quilted knickers.*
RIGHT: *Goose Goslin.*

RICKEY HENDERSON

If a ballplayer's job is strictly to get on base and score, then Rickey Henderson is the best ballplayer ever. In 25 entertaining seasons with nine teams, Henderson devastated opposing pitchers and defenses with his speed. His 1982 single-season record of 130 steals was part of a career total of 1,406 that's pretty much unapproachable. That speed helped him score an all-time high 2,295 runs, while he had enough pop to set a mark for leading off games with a homer with 81. The 1990 MVP, Rickey brought flair, style, and ego to the game. But as they say, it's not bragging if you can back it up. Rickey could.

RALPH KINER

A back problem limited Kiner to only 10 seasons, but he made the most of them. While with the Pittsburgh Pirates, he led the NL in homers in each of the first seven seasons of his career, something no other player has done. At home in "Kiner's Korner," he was later a beloved longtime broadcaster with the New York Mets.

STAN MUSIAL

For many fans, the best part about the 2009 All-Star Game in St. Louis was the appearance of the ultimate Cardinals player: Stan "The Man" Musial. As he handed the game ball to President Obama before the first pitch, Musial was able to bask in cheers earned from a life of nearly unmatched excellence on the field; his kindness and strong reputation off the field were equally notable. A seven-time NL batting champ, his 3,630 hits are fourth-most all-time, and he had enough power to club 475 homers and win six slugging titles. Musial helped the Cardinals win three World Series, and played in a whopping 24 All-Star Games.

TOP: Rickey Henderson stole even when everyone in the park knew that he was going to take off running.
LEFT: Ralph Kiner corkscrewed into his follow-through for this pregame shot.

TIM RAINES

This "Rock" could really roll . . . around the bases, that is. Raines was one of the top base stealers of the 1980s, leading the NL four times, including a career-high 90 in 1983. Of course, you have to get on base first, and Raines was a consistent .300 hitter, including an NL-best .334 in 1986. He played the bulk of his career with the Montreal Expos, followed by stints with the White Sox and Yankees before wrapping up with three other clubs. A seven-time All-Star, he was a constant weapon on the bases, with eight 50-steal seasons, and retired fifth all-time with 808 steals.

RIGHT: Stan Musial actually began his baseball career as a pitcher but was moved to the outfield in the minor leagues.
BELOW: Tim Raines

AL SIMMONS

If Al Simmons had played for, say, the Yankees, he'd be better known. As it was, he played for underachieving teams, with the notable exception of three Athletics' pennant winners (1929–1931). Though he used an unorthodox batting style that earned him the famous "Bucketfoot Al" nickname, he hit .300 or better in 13 seasons, including the first 11 of his career, had six seasons of better than 200 hits, and had 100 RBIs 12 times.

ZACK WHEAT

Few players were as connected to the Brooklyn Dodgers in the decades before World War II as Zack Wheat. The Missouri native was "adopted" by his Brooklyn neighbors and honored for 18 great seasons with the Dodgers (he ended his career in 1927 with a season with the Athletics). Wheat remains the Dodgers' franchise all-time leader in hits, games, and at-bats. He was also the 1918 NL batting champ.

LEFT Al Simmons was a key part of the Athletics' three straight AL pennant winners.
BELOW: Zack Wheat was among the greatest Dodgers players.

BILLY WILLIAMS

Playing for the Cubs alongside Ernie Banks, Billy Williams just did his job . . . over and over. He's sixth on the all-time consecutive games–played list. In 13 straight seasons, from his Rookie of the Year campaign in 1961 through 1973, he had at least 20 homers and 80 RBIs. Williams was not spectacular, but few players performed at such a solid level for so long.

BELOW: Billy Williams played in at least 157 games each year from 1962 through 1971.

TED
WILLIAMS

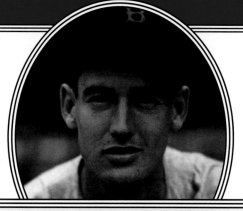

· THE SPLENDID SPLINTER ·

Ted Williams set a goal for himself when he was a young man. Many people set goals; it's the rare person who meets his so exactly. Williams famously wanted people to look at him and know that "there goes the greatest hitter who ever lived." Well, talent and hard work let him (arguably) fulfill that goal. One of the greatest pure hitters ever, Williams tortured AL pitchers for 19 seasons, while putting sportswriters and fans through the ringers as well. He just could not explain with words and attitudes what it took to be him, and how hard he worked at becoming who he was. And once he became that person, that unique, stubborn, my-way-or-the-highway man, he lived most comfortably with himself. The world just never quite knew what to do with Ted Williams.

A California native, "Teddy Ballgame" took his love of hitting to the big leagues in Boston in 1939, arriving brash and bold. He soon set a rookie record with 145 RBIs. By 1941, he reached his famous .406 average and won the first of his six batting titles (the last of which came in 1958, when he was 40). He is one of only two players to win a pair of Triple Crowns, and his two MVP trophies could probably have been doubled if writers had not used their votes to declaim his personality instead of award his skill (he finished second four times). He led the AL in on-base percentage 12 times (his career total of .482 is best ever) and slugging nine times. Only parts of five seasons lost to the military kept him from 3,000 hits, but he still found time to whack 521 homers.

But even as he put up numbers for the ages, his bitter relations with press and fans alike soured him and those around him. He craved only excellence and rarely cared what that meant to anyone else. He excelled in the military, flying planes in two wars. He excelled in fishing, becoming world-class in several disciplines. He excelled in hitting, of course. In relationships, well, it took until the end of his life before the crust began to flake off on both sides. By the time he was honored at the 1999 All-Star Game in Boston, "The Splendid Splinter" was truly beloved.

CAREER STATS:

YEARS:	19
HR:	521
RBI:	1,839
AVG:	.344

OPPOSITE: *Few players have ever devoted so much time and energy to the study of hitting as Ted Williams, who even wrote a book called* The Science of Hitting.

The Hall of Fame Field

★ ★ ★

Many teams have traditions of excellence and a parade of Hall of Famers. But only one team can claim that a trio of Hall of Fame players patrolled the same position for five decades. That team would be the Boston Red Sox, and the position would be left field.

It started in 1939 with **TED WILLIAMS** (see page 136), who terrorized AL pitchers and aggravated Boston writers until he retired in 1960. Stepping into such shoes might have ruined a young star's career, but not if that young player had the grit and gumption of **CARL "YAZ" YASTRZEMSKI** (below). Yaz moved into left field in Fenway Park and proceeded to outdo Williams as a fielder. Though not blessed with sterling athletic skills, Yaz was a worker and a grinder. He turned fielding the Green Monster into an art, leading the AL in assists seven times and tied for an eighth. At the plate, he slowly added power to an already solid (three AL batting titles) swing. In fact, he was the first AL player ever to top 3,000 hits and 400 homers in a career. And in 1967, he helped turn a losing team into a pennant winner. In the "Impossible Dream" summer, Yaz won the Triple Crown and topped off Boston's regular season by going 7-for-8 in a pair of must-win games. Though he played some DH and first base later in his career, Yaz is forever linked to the outfield in Boston.

As Yaz slowed and began to play first, the Sox turned to the third of this Hall of Fame trio. **JIM RICE** took over as the regular left fielder in 1978 and promptly won the AL MVP award. He patrolled the position for almost ten years, becoming one of the most feared sluggers in the league.

From Teddy Ballgame in 1939, through Yaz, and ending with Rice, the progression of excellence on that patch of green in Boston is unmatched in baseball.

CENTER FIELDERS

RICHIE ASHBURN

If it was pitched, he could probably hit it (two NL batting titles, nine seasons over .300) and if it was in the air, he could probably catch it (led the NL nine times in putouts). Baseball stat maven Bill James has called the fleet-footed Ashburn the best-fielding outfielder of all time. Ashburn's all-around play helped the "Whiz Kid" Phillies win the 1950 NL pennant.

RIGHT: Cool Papa's speed was legendary.
BELOW: Richie Ashburn shows off his base-running style.

JAMES "COOL PAPA" BELL

When your legendary speed is the source of the "so fast he could flip the switch and be in bed before the room got dark" line, the facts blur . . . much as he did when he rounded the bases in record time. Cool Papa Bell was once timed at a full second faster around the bases than the fastest white Major Leaguer of the day. Bell used that speed and a solid batting stroke to star in the Negro Leagues and Cuban baseball for more than two decades.

OSCAR CHARLESTON

Charleston could do it all on a baseball field, just not on a Major League field. The man that some fellow Negro Leaguers remember as the best all-around player in their game was a five-tool player in the truest sense. A powerful hitter, he was also an unmatched center fielder and a fleet base-runner. Charleston hopped from team to team, following the money, and also played in Cuba. Through it all, he was perhaps the most feared hitter in black baseball.

TY COBB

Focus on the record 11 AL batting titles, on the fourth-most all-time 897 steals, on the second-most all-time runs and hits, on the lifetime-average record .367. Pay homage to the best outfielder in the first 75 years of baseball, one of the inaugural members of the Hall of Fame. You can't tell the story of Tyrus Raymond Cobb without at least noting the personal demons that drove him to excesses of temper and anger, that tore away friends and teammates, that caused almost as much heartbreak as his talent created cheers. Nor can you tell it without being awed, plain and simple, by his all-around talent.

TOP: Oscar Charleston
BELOW: Ty Cobb's approach to the game
extended to his all-out base-running style.

JOE DIMAGGIO

As modern fans, we look back at the long history of baseball and wish that we had had a bleacher seat to watch many of the heroes. One player in particular is always described in such a way that his stats and the stories just don't seem to provide the whole picture. Joe DiMaggio played with grace, and that's something that just has to be witnessed to be fully appreciated. The record is clear: his amazing 56-game hitting streak, his .325 career average, his three MVP awards, his nine World Series rings. His accomplishments are many. But the essence of "The Yankee Clipper" was the fluid way he played.

LARRY DOBY

Along with Buzz Aldrin and John Adams, Larry Doby is destined forever for number-two status, and that's too bad. Cleveland's Doby was the first African American to play in the American League, but he followed Brooklyn's Jackie Robinson's joining the National League by four months, so he doesn't often get the credit he deserves. As a player, Doby was a homer-hitting (two times an AL leader), seven-time All-Star. As a person, he was a soft-spoken man who relished playing much more than crowing about any of his pioneering accolades.

HUGH DUFFY

This is a great connection. In 1894, Hugh Duffy hit .440 for the Boston Beaneaters, still the highest single-season average in baseball history. Almost fifty years later, after a Hall of Fame career with six teams in which he built a reputation as one of the finest fielders of his day, Duffy was a coach with the Red Sox. One of his pupils was the last man to reach that magic .400 mark, Ted Williams. A great story of the continuity of baseball wisdom.

*TOP: **Joe DiMaggio***
*ABOVE: **Hugh Duffy***
*RIGHT: **Powerhouse Larry Doby fielding for the Indians.***

KEN GRIFFEY JR.

Few players ran to the field with such visible joy as this fleet-footed slugging lefty. Griffey put the Seattle Mariners on his back—and on the map—with a remarkable 1995 season that saw them beat the mighty Yankees in the ALDS. Griffey himself slid home with the walk-off winning run. "The Kid" was a 13-time All-Star and the 1997 AL MVP when he cracked a career-best-tying 56 bombs. That was one of four times he led the league in round-trippers on his way to seventh place all-time with 630 homers. His wall-climbing outfield ability earned him 10 Gold Gloves, among the most ever at the position. In 1990, "Junior" had the unique thrill of playing in the same outfield as his dad, three-time All-Star Ken Griffey, Sr. The pair also became the first father-son duo to hit back-to-back homers in a game. He was elected with 99.3 percent of the Hall of Fame vote, at the time an all-time record.

KIRBY PUCKETT

Come game time, there was no love lost between Kirby Puckett and the pitchers who faced him. But even then, they probably only disliked him during the game. Fans made him a 10-time All-Star, though he made it an easy choice by leading the AL in hits four times and winning six Gold Gloves in center. He led the Twins to World Series titles in 1987 and 1991. His Game Six exploits (memorable 3rd-inning catch, game-winning homer) in '91 are all-time Series highlights. A .318 career hitter, his time in baseball was cut short by glaucoma in 1995 and in life by heart disease in 2006.

TRIS SPEAKER

Speaker could have earned his Hall of Fame spot by either his defense or his offense, since both were so far superior to most of those around him. A master of dead-ball hitting, he led the AL in doubles eight times while compiling a .345 lifetime average, still sixth all-time. On defense, the "Grey Eagle" was famous for playing so shallow that he could occasionally make plays at second base. He used this style to set an all-time record for outfield assists with 450. Speaker was a key part of Boston's three World Series triumphs in the years before and during World War I.

TOP LEFT: Kirby Puckett
TOP RIGHT: Tris Speaker
OPPOSITE: Ken Griffey Jr.

TOP LEFT: Lloyd Waner played on the same Major League team with his brother and fellow Hall of Famer Paul for 15 seasons.
TOP RIGHT: Hack Wilson's 56 homers in 1930 were the NL record until Mark McGwire hit 70 in 1998.
LEFT: Turkey Stearnes was elected to the Hall of Fame in 2000.

LLOYD WANER

When "Little Poison" went to the plate, he was going to put the bat on the ball. Waner struck out only once in every 45 at-bats, and he also never walked more than 40 times in a season. It must have worked, since he had 223 hits as a rookie in 1927 while hitting .355, third behind his brother, outfield teammate, and fellow future Hall of Famer Paul. A .316 career hitter, Lloyd used his speed to great effect in patrolling center field and legging out hits.

HACK WILSON

At first glance, Wilson might seem to be a one-year wonder, a man whose mark of 191 RBIs (helped by 56 homers) in 1930 remains a single-season record. (And, in fact, the closest anyone has come since World War II ended was the 165 RBIs by Manny Ramirez of Cleveland in 1999.) But from 1926 to 1932, the Cubs' big-armed basher was consistently one of the top RBI men and sluggers in the NL. His bulging biceps created a swift, powerful stroke.

TURKEY STEARNES

Norman Stearnes got the nickname "Turkey" after kids saw him running in a way that reminded them of the bird. All grown up, Turkey got his spot in the Hall of Fame for a 25-year Negro League career, spanning from 1920 to 1945, as one of the game's top hitters. His career average was above .350, according to most reports.

Willie, Mickey, and the Duke

To a generation of New York City baseball fans, they were already three of the most famous and beloved players of all time. But then a musician named Terry Cashman wrote a song in 1981 that immortalized the trio for generations to come.

WILLIE MAYS, of course, was a legend, a superstar of the New York Giants. More about the Say-Hey Kid on page 146.

A superstar of the Yankees, **MICKEY "THE MICK" MANTLE** (below) was a somewhat tragic hero. Seemingly destined to an earth-shattering career, knee injuries early in his baseball life slowed his marvelous speed but didn't stop his thundering bat. Mantle set a record for homers by a switch-hitter with 536, leading the AL four times and winning three MVP awards. Though he looked like he was always in pain, his game smile and country charm—to say nothing of the seven World Series he helped the Bombers win—endeared him to a city.

One part of that city, however, had a different hero. The Duke of Flatbush, **EDWIN "DUKE" SNIDER**, had more home runs in the 1950s than any other player, Willie and Mickey be darned. He had six seasons with 100 or more RBI, including a league-leading 136 in 1955. That, of course, was the magic season in which Duke and Pee Wee and Jackie and the rest brought the World Series title home to Brooklyn for the first and only time. For Brooklynites, Cashman's song only cemented Snider's already immortal status.

They made their legends on the field; Cashman put their deeds—and the spirit of those wonderful times—to music.

WILLIE MAYS

• THE FIVE-TOOL PLAYER •

He had the power to send some 660 baseballs into the seats . . . His speed made him one of fewer than five players with 300 steals and 500 homers . . . His defensive skills won him 12 Gold Gloves and acclaim as probably the best ever to play center . . . He had 3,283 hits, six top-three finishes in NL batting races, and played in a whopping 24 All-Star Games . . . And on top of all that, he modeled an infectious enthusiasm, a boyish glee at playing a boys' game, and a joie de vivre the lifted spirits all around. The scoreboard totals don't lie: There just was never another ballplayer like Willie Mays.

The "Say-Hey Kid" (a nickname picked up from his own oft-used greeting) was one in more than a million, combining all of baseball's key offensive and defensive skills at higher combined levels than any other player. He was, as they say today, the total package, a consummate baseball

CAREER STATS:	
YEARS:	22
HR:	660
RBI:	1,903
AVG:	.320

player who excelled at the highest levels and played for more than two decades. A Rookie of the Year at 20 in 1951, he was an MVP when he was 23 and again when he was 34. He topped 50 homers in 1955 and again in 1965. He helped the New York Giants win the 1954 World Series, and 17 years later led the NL in on-base percentage while helping the San Francisco Giants win the NL West.

Cap flying, wall crashing, bowlegs churning, Mays ate up a baseball field, whether covering ground in the outfield or dirt on the base paths. And the fans ate him up in return, making him one of the most beloved figures in the game.

Of course, we have to mention The Catch, his memorable moment in the '54 Series, when he saved Game One. After a long run to an over-the-shoulder catch 420 feet from home, he spun and threw to keep runners from scoring. Best part about that famous play? Willie says he made lots of others that were better!

ABOVE: *Willie Mays shows off the powerful throwing arm that was just one part of his arsenal of baseball skills.*

PLAYER'S CONTRACT

Compare this contract signed by Willie Mays in 1963 to the much simpler form
signed by Lou Gehrig in 1926 . . . and compare the dollar amounts!

UNIFORM PLAYER'S CONTRACT

National League of Professional Baseball Clubs

Parties   Between   San Francisco Giants Base Ball Club

herein called the Club, and   Willie Howard Mays, Jr.,

of 54 Mendosa Ave., San Francisco, Cal. herein called the Player.

Recital   The Club is a member of the National League of Professional Baseball Clubs, a voluntary association of ten member clubs which has subscribed to the Major League Rules with the American League of Professional Baseball Clubs and its constituent clubs and to the Professional Baseball Rules with that League and the National Association of Baseball Leagues. The purpose of those rules is to insure the public wholesome and high-class professional baseball by defining the relations between Club and Player, between club and club, between league and league, and by vesting in a designated Commissioner broad powers of control and discipline, and of decision in case of disputes.

Agreement   In consideration of the facts above recited and of the promises of each to the other, the parties agree as follows:

Employment   1. The Club hereby employs the Player to render, and the Player agrees to render, skilled services as a baseball player during the year _____ 1963 including the Club's training season, the Club's exhibition games, the Club's playing season, and the World Series (or any other official series in which the Club may participate and in any receipts of which the player may be entitled to share).

Payment   2. For performance of the Player's services and promises hereunder the Club will pay the Player the sum of 105,000.00 (One Hundred, Five Thousand Dollars) and _____

hereof _____ unless the Player is "abroad" with the Club for the purpose of playing games, in which event the amount then due shall be paid on the first week-day after the return "home" of the Club, the terms "home" and "abroad" meaning respectively at and away from the city in which the Club has its baseball field.

If a monthly rate of payment is stipulated above, it shall begin with the commencement of the Club's playing season (or such subsequent date as the Player's services may commence) and end with the termination of the Club's scheduled playing season, and shall be payable in semi-monthly installments as above provided.

If the player is in the service of the Club for part of the playing season only, he shall receive such proportion of the sum above mentioned, as the number of days of his actual employment in the Club's playing season bears to the number of days in said season.

Notwithstanding the rate of payment stipulated above, the minimum rate of payment to the Player for each day of service on a Major League Club shall be at the rate of $6,000 per year; except that such minimum rate of payment shall be at the rate of $7,000 per year retroactive to the beginning of the season if the Player is on a Major League Club's roster on June 15 and shall be at the rate of $7,000 per year if the Player physically joins a Major League Club between June 15 and August 31. If a player physically joins a Major League Club on or after September 1, the minimum rate of payment shall be at the rate of $6,000 per year for each day of service with such Major League Club.

Loyalty   3. (a) The Player agrees to perform his services hereunder diligently and faithfully, to keep himself in first class physical condition and to obey the Club's training rules, and pledges himself to the American public and to the Club to conform to high standards of personal conduct, fair play and good sportsmanship.

Baseball Promotion   (b) In addition to his services in connection with the actual playing of baseball, the Player agrees to cooperate with the Club and participate in any and all promotional activities of the Club or its League, which, in the opinion of the Club, will promote the welfare of the Club or professional baseball, and to observe and comply with all requirements of the Club respecting conduct and service of its teams and its players, at all times whether on or off the field.

Pictures and Public Appearances   (c) The Player agrees that his picture may be taken for still photographs, motion pictures or television at such times as the Club may designate and agrees that all rights in such pictures shall belong to the Club and may be used by the Club for publicity purposes in any manner it desires. The Player further agrees that during the playing season he will not make public appearances, participate in radio or television programs or permit his picture to be taken or write or sponsor newspaper or magazine articles or sponsor commercial products without the written consent of the Club, which shall not be withheld except in the reasonable interests of the Club or professional baseball.

Player Representations / Ability   4. (a) The Player represents and agrees that he has exceptional and unique skill and ability as a baseball player; that his services to be rendered hereunder are of a special, unusual and extraordinary character which gives them peculiar value which cannot be reasonably or adequately compensated for in damages at law, and that the Player's breach of this contract will cause the Club great and irreparable injury and damage. The Player agrees that, in addition to other remedies, the Club shall be entitled to injunctive and other equitable relief to prevent a breach of this contract by the Player, including, among others, the right to enjoin the Player from playing baseball for any other person or organization during the term of this contract.

Condition   (b) The Player represents that he has no physical or mental defects, known to him, which would prevent or impair performance of his services.

Interest in Club   (c) The Player represents that he does not, directly or indirectly, own stock or have any financial interest in the ownership or earnings of any Major League club, except as hereinafter expressly set forth, and covenants that he will not hereafter, while connected with any Major League club, acquire or hold any such stock or interest except in accordance with Major League Rule 20 (e).

Service   5. (a) The Player agrees that, while under contract, and prior to expiration of the Club's right to renew this contract, he will not play baseball otherwise than for the Club, except that the Player may participate in post-season games under the conditions prescribed in the Major League Rules. Major League Rule 18 (b) is set forth on page 4 hereof.

_____ additional 800 miles.

Post-Season Exhibition Games. Major League Rule 18 (b) provides:

Exhibition Games. (b) No Player shall participate in any exhibition game played during the period between the close of the Major League championship season and the following training season; except that a Player, with the written consent of the Commissioner, may participate in exhibition games which are played within thirty days after the close of the Major League championship season and which are approved by the Commissioner. Player conduct, on and off the field, in connection with such post-season exhibition games shall be subject to the discipline of the Commissioner. The Commissioner shall not approve more than three Players of any one Club on the same team. No Player shall participate in any exhibition game with or against any team which, during the current season or within one year, has had any ineligible player or which is or has been during the current season or within one year, managed and controlled by an ineligible player or by any person who has listed an ineligible player under an assumed name or who otherwise has violated, or attempted to violate, any exhibition game contract; or with or against any team which, during said season or within one year, has played against teams containing such ineligible players, or so managed or controlled. Any player violating this rule shall be fined not less than fifty dollars ($50) nor more than five hundred dollars ($500), except that in no event shall such fine be less than the consideration received by such player for participating in such game.

PROCLAMATION

In 1979, Willie Mays was inducted into the Hall of Fame. His adopted home city of San Francisco honored him as well, with this proclamation.

OFFICE OF THE MAYOR
SAN FRANCISCO

DIANNE FEINSTEIN

Proclamation

WHEREAS, Willie Mays, the "Say Hey, Kid," is a shining legend in the annals of baseball and is universally recognized as one of the world's most gifted athletes; and

WHEREAS, More than two-thirds of Willie Mays' remarkable achievements, including 14 years in a 22-year professional baseball career, occurred here in San Francisco, from 1958, when the Giants moved from New York to San Francisco, representing the game's Westward Migration, until his return to New York in 1972; and

WHEREAS, During Willie Mays' 14 years as a San Francisco Giant, this incredible athlete was amassing such remarkable baseball records as a career total of more than 3,000 base hits, 660 home runs, a lifetime batting average of .302, and more than 7,000 catches in the outfield—a record that no baseball player is ever likely to match or to exceed; and

WHEREAS, These records and the tremendous playing performance that Willie Mays always delivered made him baseball's outstanding attraction, and led to his election to baseball's Hall of Fame at Cooperstown, New York, in January, 1979, by the largest vote total in the Hall of Fame's history, indicating clearly that Willie Mays is still breaking records; and

WHEREAS, Wille Mays will be inducted officially into baseball's Hall of Fame on Sunday, August 5, 1979, and that many experts believe that Willie Mays may well have been the greatest baseball player in the history of the sport, now

THEREFORE, BE IT RESOLVED, THAT I, Dianne Feinstein, Mayor of the City and County of San Francisco, do hereby proclaim Sunday, August 5, 1979, as WILLIE MAYS DAY in order to honor and to pay homage to one of our City's most gifted athletes and most outstanding citizens, and as a way to express our gratitude to him for his enormous contributions to San Francisco's sports fans, to the youth of our community, and to the game of baseball. BE IT FURTHER RESOLVED that I commend all San Franciscans to join with me in celebrating the recognition of a man, and an athlete, who shared his superb talents and interests with our City for many, many years.

IN WITNESS WHEREOF, I have hereunto set my hand and caused the Seal of the City and County of San Francisco to be affixed this thirty-first day of July, nineteen hundred and seventy-nine.

Dianne Feinstein
Mayor

RIGHT FIELDERS

HANK AARON

No player has ever been as sure and steady as the great Hank Aaron was, topping 30 homers in 15 seasons and besting 90 RBIs in 16 seasons (he's still the all-time champ in career RBI with 2,297). He earned All-Star selections every year from 1955 through 1975. Aaron just performed, over and over. That steady performance stood him in good stead in 1974 when he battled NL pitchers and racist taunts as he overtook Babe Ruth to become the all-time home-run leader. Aaron has gone on to be a leader off the field as a team executive and community leader. Though his record of 755 has been topped by Barry Bonds, Aaron remains No. 1 in many fans' hearts.

ANDRE DAWSON

"The Hawk" waited a long time to take his rightful place in Cooperstown, but his 2010 election was worth the wait. The all-around star is one of only five players with 400 career homers and 300 career steals (joined by Willie Mays, Barry Bonds, Carlos Beltran, and Alex Rodrieguez). Dawson was the NL Rookie of the Year for the Expos and braved Montreal's rock-hard turf for 11 seasons. Though the pounding took a toll on his knees, he battled on. A move to the grass in Wrigley in 1987 led to his NL MVP award and new life for his career. With eight Gold Gloves and four Silver Sluggers, Dawson was a dynamo.

VLADIMIR GUERRERO

Guerrero never saw a pitch he couldn't hit. The Dominican native was a nine-time All-Star and the 2004 AL MVP with the Angels. He starred for the Expos for eight years before moving to the AL. He became a consistent RBI man for the Halos, with four 100-plus seasons including a career-high 126 in his MVP season. Guerrero also had a powerful throwing arm that runners rarely challenged. For his Anaheim heroics—he helped the Halos reach the playoffs five times in his six seasons there—Guerrero became the first Hall player to wear an Angels cap on his Cooperstown plaque.

TOP: After his playing days with the Braves were over, Hank Aaron moved into a key front-office position.
LEFT: Tony Gwynn was a magician with a bat, consistently finding a way to succeed.

TONY GWYNN

Tony Gwynn used a baseball bat like Leonard Bernstein used a baton or Julia Child used a mixing spoon. They were all masters at work, seemingly able to produce beauty and success amid just about any circumstance. Gwynn's eight NL titles are tied for most in that league. The 15-time All-Star had five seasons with 200 hits, and though he never won a World Series ring, he will always be Mr. Padre.

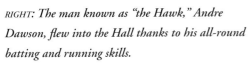

RIGHT: *The man known as "the Hawk," Andre Dawson, flew into the Hall thanks to his all-round batting and running skills.*
BELOW: *Vladimir Guerrero*

REGGIE JACKSON

Man, could Reggie hit the ball a long way. His 563 homers more than made up for his all-time record 2,597 strikeouts. And his powerful personality was offset by his ability to carry a team to titles, which he did three times with Oakland and twice with the Yankees. And no one earned his nickname with more drama: After hitting three homers on three straight pitches in the 1977 World Series, Jackson became Mr. October forevermore.

AL KALINE

You might call Kaline the quiet superstar. He was a sure and steady force for the Tigers for 22 years, highlighted by their 1968 World Series title. He never led the AL in homers or RBI and had just one batting title. But he was a 15-time All-Star, a 10-time Gold Glove winner, and a member of the 3,000-hit club (plus missed the 400-homer club by just one!). Kaline's quiet success doesn't get all the headlines, but Tigers fans know he's one of the all-time greats.

WILLIE KEELER

Though he was smaller than most of today's batboys (hence his nickname, "Wee Willie"), Keeler is a baseball immortal. He earned his lasting fame for one of baseball's most treasured sayings—"Hit 'em where they ain't"—and for living up to that phrase. Playing 19 seasons (1892–1910), he put together a .341 lifetime average and an NL-record 44-game hitting streak. His record of eight straight seasons with at least 200 hits was not passed until 2009 by Ichiro Suzuki. . . and the advice to hitters contained in Keeler's famous saying is still used by coaches from Little League on up.

TOP: *Reggie Jackson*

LEFT: *The highlight of Al Kaline's long and successful career with the Tigers was surely the team's 1968 World Series championship.*

CHUCK KLEIN

On the list of all-time sluggers, Klein's is one name that escapes some fans' notice. Not to say he didn't do his part: four NL home run crowns, the 1933 NL Triple Crown, four seasons with 120 or more RBI, and a four-homer game in 1936. He played 17 seasons, mostly with the Phillies (for whom he got that Triple Crown), but also spent time with the Cubs and Pirates.

TOP: Chuck Klein's Triple Crown stats in 1933: .368 average, 28 homers, and 120 RBIs.
RIGHT: Willie Keeler

ABOVE: Mel Ott demonstrates the high leg kick
he used effectively as a timing mechanism.
ABOVE RIGHT: Frank Robinson

MEL OTT

Ott got off to a fast start and never looked back. The Giants slugger had 42 homers in 1928 when he was just 20 years old. By the time he retired in 1947, he had 511 homers—at the time, the most ever by a National Leaguer. He'd also earned six NL home-run titles. His high-kick left-handed batting stroke was perfect for the short porch of the Polo Grounds, which, combined with his famous "nice guy" personality, made him a fan favorite.

FRANK ROBINSON

Frank Robinson earned just about every important award you can think of: Rookie of the Year, MVP in both the AL and the NL, the last NL Triple Crown in 1966, a Gold Glove, World Series rings in 1966 and 1970, 586 homers, and 12 All-Star nods. On that alone, he's one of the most accomplished players of the past five decades. In 1975, however, he made history when he became the first African American manager of a Major League team, taking over as player-manager for the Cleveland Indians.

LARRY WALKER

This Canadian native could rake with the best of them. Larry Walker combined wall-bashing power with league-leading batting-average skills in a 17-year big-league career. After starting his career with the Expos, he really flourished after moving to Colorado. With the Rockies, he led the NL in batting average three times. His .379 career-best in 1999 was one of four seasons at .350 or above. He also topped the senior circuit with 49 homers in 1997, when he was named the NL MVP. Add in seven 15-plus-steal seasons and 154 outfield assists and you've got a five-tool Hall of Famer.

PAUL WANER

He got the nickname "Big Poison" from a Brooklyn fan who mangled the word "person," but he was poison for NL pitchers. He hit .333 in 20 seasons and topped 200 hits eight times, all adding up to more than 3,000 career hits. He also enjoyed playing alongside his brother Lloyd ("Little Poison") for 13 years in Pittsburgh.

DAVE WINFIELD

Winfield might just be the most talented all-around athlete in the Hall. Not only did he pitch the University of Minnesota to a College World Series title, he was drafted by the NBA, the ABA, and the NFL. He was so ready for the bigs that he's one of the few modern players to skip the minors entirely. He had his best seasons with the Padres and Yankees, and put the capper on a great career with a World Series-winning double for the Blue Jays in the 1992 World Series. The next year, he became a member of the 3,000-hit club, finishing his Hall of Fame career with 3,110 hits.

ABOVE: Dave Winfield used his great athletic skills to help three teams win.

Designated for the Hall

The designated hitter has been part of baseball (well . . . AL baseball!) since 1973. The position began as a sort of add-on for backup outfielders or late-career sluggers. It evolved into a potent offensive weapon, which of course led to some players far exceeding others. The Hall's voters recognized this and inducted a pair of players who made their livings with their bats alone (for the most part!).

EDGAR MARTINEZ (above left) so firmly established the level of excellence for DHs that the annual award for the top DH is named for him. A Mariners star for 18 seasons, his smooth righthanded stroke was as dependable as the Seattle tides. Originally a third baseman, Martinez put aside his glove starting in 1995 and flourished. He was a two-time AL batting champ and had a .312 career mark.

HAROLD BAINES (above right) did spend more time in the field than Martinez, with more than 1,000 ABs an outfielder, but it was as a hitter that he really made his biggest mark. The dependable lefty racked up 2,866 hits over 22 years, primarily with the White Sox and Orioles. And he made them count, knocking in 1,628 runs.

ROBERTO CLEMENTE

· SEÑOR BÉISBOL ·

There's a bridge in Pittsburgh, a statue near the ballpark, a U.S. postage stamp, and an annual award given by Major League Baseball. There are dozens of fields and ballparks in many countries. They all bear his name: Roberto Clemente. But Clemente's greatest legacy is not his name, but what he did for his people and his sport. As the first superstar from Latin America, Clemente was, in a very real way, a trailblazer in the mold of Jackie Robinson. Look around the game today and imagine what it would be like without the stunning talent that flows in a horsehide stream from the Caribbean Sea.

Clemente grew up in Puerto Rico and was a star player early, performing for sugar-mill teams and then for the Santurce Cangrejeros. Signed by the Dodgers in an early bid to tap the Caribbean market, he was snaked by the Pirates a year later in a great roster maneuver and arrived in Pittsburgh in 1955. He struggled early on to adapt his speed and skills to the big-league game, though he did hit .311 in his second season. And he struggled, too, with life away from the field. A kid from a faraway island, he faced many of the prejudices faced by African American players.

But talent like Clemente's could not stay down forever. By 1960, he hit .314 and helped the Pirates win the World Series. The next year, he won the first of his four batting titles and the first of his record 12 straight Gold Gloves (he's still regarded as having one of the best throwing arms of all time). The 1966 NL MVP, he carried the Pirates back to the Series in 1971, batting .414 and hitting two homers, including one in Game Seven.

As his skills brought him fame, he brought a message of unity and hope to Spanish-speaking lands all over. His generosity was legendary and he gave tirelessly of his time and energy. In his last at-bat of the 1972 season, he got his 3,000th hit, the first Latin player to reach that mark.

Sadly, while shepherding a cache of relief supplies to earthquake-hit Nicaragua in December 1972, he was killed in a plane crash. Clemente's real legacy? Just think of it the next time someone asks you for help.

CAREER STATS:	
YEARS:	18
HR:	240
RBI:	1,305
AVG:	.317
H:	3,000

*OPPOSITE: **Roberto Clemente's slashing stroke carved out 3,000 career hits and helped him win four NL batting titles.***

MEMBERSHIP CARD

Kids of all backgrounds were drawn to Roberto Clemente's cap-flying, all-out-hustle style. This card was for one of his fan clubs.

MEMBERSHIP CARD

ROBERTO CLEMENTE FAN CLUB

Name _____

Send for latest FREE 8 x 10 Full Color Picture of Roberto Clemente suitable for framing. Send to Roberto Clemente Fan Club, P.O. Box 2100, Pittsburgh, Pa. 15230. Enclose 25c for postage and handling.

N. Y. Friends of Roberto Clemente

ABOVE AND RIGHT: Trailblazer Roberto Clemente.

SCORESHEET

Not only is this a historic document, the scoresheet showing Clemente's 3000th hit (and signed by Clemente), it's also a great look at how baseball stats were compiled, one game at a time by diligent official scorers.

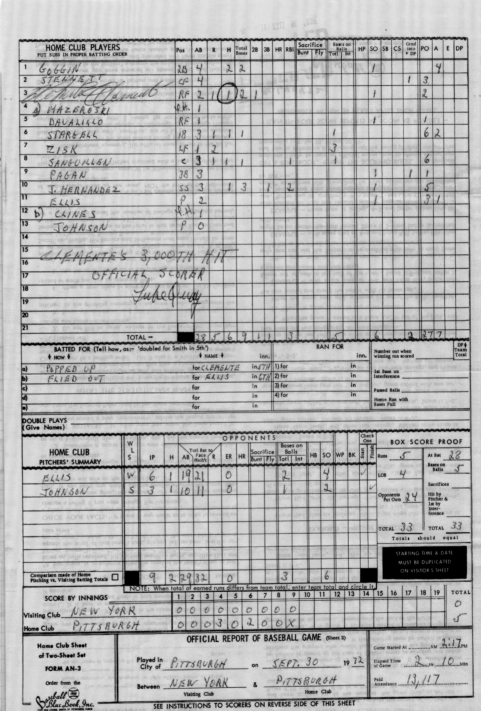

5

THE MANAGERS

The leaders of baseball teams hold a couple of unique places in the world of sports. They are (at least in America) the only ones known as managers: football and basketball teams are run by coaches. Baseball managers are also the only such people required to dress in the same uniform as their charges, hewing to the still-extant rule that anyone entering the field of play (in a non-medical way) must be in uniform. More recently than in most sports, too, managers doubled as players: the last man to act as a player-manager was the Reds' Pete Rose in 1986.

In uniform or out, as former players or not, the men who have risen to the level of Hall of Fame manager have some shared characteristics. Longevity, for one, though that might be said to come as a result of some of their other attributes: leadership ability, inspirational quality, a powerful personality. The men in these pages and in the Hall were innovative, stubborn, smart, personable, frosty, nice, or mean . . . as the situation dictated. Steering players to succeed remains as much an alchemy as a set of marching, or playing, orders. Behold the wizards.

OPPOSITE: Quiet determination on the face of Joe McCarthy.

ABOVE: *Pittsburgh favorite Ned Hanlon in an 1887 photo.*
OPPOSITE: *This photo shows John McGraw visiting a ballpark later in his life. When managing, he wore the team uniform.*

MAKING THE MODERN MANAGER

Though men like Harry Wright were well-known and successful leaders before him, **NED HANLON** helped establish the role of the modern manager. Hanlon took over a struggling Baltimore Orioles club in the National League in 1892. Gathering a group of tough, win-at-all-costs, likeminded players around him, Hanlon's O's eventually dominated the league. Six of his players from these teams would join him in the Hall of Fame eventually. By 1894, they were league champs for the first of three straight years. Hanlon and the Orioles were celebrated for their "little ball" style, while his own ideas about platooning were years ahead of their time. It was a rowdy, scrappy, rough game and the Orioles played it better than any. Hanlon later gutted the Orioles when they merged with Brooklyn, for whom he was both manager and president—and pennant winner again.

LITTLE NAPOLEON

JOHN MCGRAW was a third baseman on Hanlon's pennant-winning Baltimore teams, and he took their pugnacious attitude with him when he became manager of the New York Giants in 1902, following three seasons as Baltimore's. He led the Giants to a pennant by 1904, though he and the Giants refused to play the AL-champion Boston team in the then-new World Series. The rivalry between the established NL and the upstart AL was much fiercer in those days. The Giants did play and win the 1905 World Series, but lost the Series four times before the end of World War I. McGraw became, in that time, better known than most of his players, a character ready with a nasty quote as often against his team as for it. In fact, until 2007, he held the all-time record for ejections with 131. He continued to lead the Giants until 1932, winning four more pennants and two more world championships. McGraw remains on the short list of baseball's greatest managers.

They Also Played

Not every manager has made it to the big leagues as a player, but many Hall of Fame managers did combine some level of playing success with winning from the dugout. Here's a quick look at the playing highlights of some Hall of Fame managers.

RUBE FOSTER	Pitcher for several teams in the Negro Leagues, including the Cuban X-Giants.
NED HANLON	(pictured below) Played with five teams; helped Detroit Wolverines win 1887 pennant.
MILLER HUGGINS	Played 13 seasons at second base; led league in walks, putouts, and assists.
JOHN MCGRAW	Helped Orioles win three pennants in 1890s; .334 career average.
CASEY STENGEL	Played outfield with several teams, including Brooklyn and Pittsburgh.

MORE THAN A MANAGER

Without the drive, ambition, and talent of **RUBE FOSTER**, the Negro Leagues might never have become such an economic and athletic success. After playing with several all-black semipro and professional teams, and succeeding wildly as a pitcher who earned his nickname as a comparison to the great Rube Waddell, Foster became a manager in 1907. He then helped form the Chicago American Giants in 1911. By 1920, he had gained enough power and influence that it was under his leadership that the Negro National League was born. He was president, organizer, team manager, and receiver of five percent of the gross. Salaries and attendance grew mightily, as did the caliber of play. Sadly, Foster grew too sick to lead and by 1926 was in the hospital; he died in 1930, his imprint on baseball assured.

TOP LEFT: Rube Foster went from the pitcher's mound to the executive offices.
TOP RIGHT: Miller Huggins had just the right personality to manage a crew of stars.

TWO MIGHTY YANKS

Sure, you might say, anyone could have won with the talent that **MILLER HUGGINS** and **JOE MCCARTHY** had. But then again, other teams with many talented players have not had the dynastic runs that the Yankees enjoyed under these two men's leadership. And maybe that's the tale: They were leaders. They were as much group psychologists as strategic wizards. Their Hall of Fame credentials were burnished not by innovation or creativity, but by an ability to blend greatness, ego, and talent into winning—far from an easy task.

Huggins took over in 1918, and, yes, two years later he was blessed with Babe Ruth. But their relationship was often frosty and occasionally ice-cold. Still, Huggins molded Ruth into a lineup that would soon include Lou Gehrig, Waite Hoyt, and other Hall of Famers. Under Huggins's leadership, New York won six pennants and three World Series. His 1927 team is considered one of the best ever. Sadly, Huggins died suddenly late in the 1929 season.

McCarthy took over in 1931 after managing the Cubs. He would hold the job for 16 years and oversee such stars as Gehrig, Joe DiMaggio, Lefty Gomez, and Joe Gordon. The Yankees of these years were a dynasty, winning seven pennants and six World Series from 1936 to 1943. McCarthy made his reputation not as a screamer, but as a quiet, determined leader.

THE OLD PERFESSOR

What can you say about **CASEY STENGEL** that he didn't probably say himself at one time or another? One of baseball's greatest characters—do you speak "Stengelese"?—his malapropisms and colorful character overshadow his record as one of the great managers. With seven World Series titles, Stengel tied McCarthy for the most ever. Only Stengel's teams have won five World Series in a row. He didn't start his managing career on the top, however. After a nice playing career as an outfielder, he managed in the minors and then nine seasons (eight of them losing) with the Dodgers and Braves (a.k.a. the Bees), and then the minors again. So it was a big surprise when the mighty Yankees made him their skipper for the 1949 season. Good choice. In the next dozen years, the Yanks won 10 pennants and seven world titles, including five in a row (1949–53). A career wrap-up stint as the Mets first (and most unsuccessful) manager again clouded his record. But cognoscenti know that in Stengelese, the word for "winner" is "Casey."

A BIRD IN THE DIRT

To be sure, **EARL WEAVER** was an inspired leader of men, a manager of innovative skill. The Earl of Baltimore led the Orioles to four AL pennants and the 1970 World Series title. His pitchers also won six Cy Young awards, a testament to his love of their crucial role and his pitching coaches' wisdom. Weaver was also quite the umpire baiter, famous for arguing, kicking dirt, tossing caps, and getting kicked out of 97 games. Amid all the yelling, he won more games than not by a long stretch—even though he didn't get to stick around to watch all of them.

TOP: *Casey Stengel's tough demeanor masked a wily baseball mind.*
LEFT: *Earl Weaver*
OPPOSITE TOP: *Walter Alston*
OPPOSITE: *Tommy Lasorda was not only a master cheerleader, he was a great help to his teams.*

DODGER BLUE

From 1954 to early 1996, the Dodgers had two managers, and both ended up in the Hall of Fame. **WALTER ALSTON** signed the first of his 23 straight one-year contracts in 1954. One year later, he helped make "next year" this year by leading the Dodgers to their only title in Brooklyn. He moved with them to Los Angeles and kept up the winning ways, bringing the Series title to the West Coast in 1959. He led them to four more pennants and two World Series titles in L.A. with an understated, softspoken style.

The same could not be said of his successor as L.A.'s skipper. Former lefty pitcher **TOMMY LASORDA** took over in 1976, ready to lead the many players he had skippered in seven years of managing in the Dodgers' minor leagues. Lasorda is a baseball lifer, a man who has spent his entire pro life in it. Famous for "bleeding Dodger blue," he is one of the greater ambassadors for the sport and his club. He often brought celebrity friends to the ballpark to spread the love. Lasorda's legendary enthusiasm comes on top of a resume that includes four NL pennants and two World Series titles. Already a Hall of Famer, having left the dugout in 1996, he capped off his career in uniform by leading the U.S. to a gold medal at the 2000 Olympic Games.

TWOFER

It takes great skill—and good timing—to lead one team to a World Series, to say nothing of carrying two teams there. **SPARKY ANDERSON** managed that with a team from each league. He was the lead mechanic of the 1975–76 Big Red Machine in Cincinnati, and later helped the Tigers roar to the title in 1984. That latter team set a record by going 35–5 out of the gate, leading wire-to-wire and winning the Tigers' first title since 1968. Chatty and personable, Anderson got along with players and media alike, but he was not afraid to mix it up with umpires when the need arose. He was also once called "Captain Hook" for his ideas about when to pull pitchers. His 2,194 wins are sixth all-time.

Only two managers can say they won a World Series with two different clubs. **TONY LA RUSSA** is one of them, and the most recent. First, he guided a powerful Oakland team to a title in 1989. After moving to the Cardinals, he led them to three Fall Classics, winning in 2006 and 2011. La Russa began his career with the White Sox in 1979 at the age of only 34, where he was the AL Manager of the Year in 1983. He moved to the Athletics in 1986 and led them for 10 years and three AL pennants. He took over the Cardinals in 1996 and starting in 2000, directed a streak of 11 winning seasons out of 12, six division titles, three NL pennants, and a pair of World Series wins. He trails only Connie Mack and John McGraw on the all-time managers wins list, pretty nice company indeed.

BOBBY COX

Over the course of the Atlanta Braves' amazing 14-year streak of NL East titles (including five NL pennants), the players came and went for the most part, but one thing was the same: Bobby Cox was in charge. He had his first big-league skipper work with the Braves from 1978–1981 and later returned to the club as GM. After four seasons running the Toronto Blue Jays, he was back in the Braves' dugout in 1990 and the title streak started the next season. The highlight of the run was the Braves' 1995 World Series triumph over Cleveland. Cox was a four-time manager of the year and ended up fourth all-time with 2,504 regular-season wins.

JOE TORRE

Torre skippered five teams—the Mets, Braves, Cardinals, Yankees, and Dodgers—but it was his amazing work with the Bronx Bombers in the late 1990s and early 2000s that cemented his Hall of Fame credentials. Torre's Yanks won four World Series from 1996 through 2000, including a team-record 114-win season in 1998. They won two more AL titles in 2001 and 2003 as well. Torre was a great player, too, winning the 1971 NL MVP as a Cards third baseman. His work as a manager, however, sent him to Cooperstown fifth all-time with 2,326 wins.

*OPPOSITE TOP: **Sparky Anderson***
*OPPOSITE LEFT: **Tony La Russa***
*OPPOSITE RIGHT: **Bobby Cox***
*RIGHT: **Joe Torre***

CONNIE
MACK

• THE GRAND OLD MAN •

I t is probably not an exaggeration to say that Connie Mack saw more baseball games than anyone in history. As the longest-tenured manager in the game, he watched his teams win 3,731 games . . . and lose 3,948. Add in his playing career and some minor league games, and you can figure that he saw in person perhaps 10,000 baseball games. That's a lot of hot dogs.

Mack started his big league baseball odyssey as a catcher in 1886, and played 11 Major League seasons with three teams. Never a star, he was nonetheless a student of the game. During his final three seasons, he was the player-manager of the Pittsburgh Pirates of the NL.

In 1901, when the American League started, Mack bought a part of one of the franchises and named himself manager. For the next half-century, through two wars, the Black Sox Scandal, the coming of Ruth, and the end of the

CAREER STATS:

GAMES:	7,755
WINS:	3,582
WORLD SERIES TITLES:	5

"color line," the one constant in baseball was Mack at the helm of the Athletics.

He was the team's owner, general manager, and field manager, though he never went on the field during games. Mack preferred to wear a business suit while on the bench. He sent coaches or other players out to make any pitching changes.

The Athletics under Mack lived in waves based on money. On at least two occasions, he slowly built championship teams only to be forced to sell the stars soon after winning. He did capture five World Series titles, though, three in the 1910s and two more in 1929–30.

How long did Mack manage? He led the A's for 13 seasons after being elected to the Hall of Fame and was uniquely, personally involved in every aspect of a Major League team. And due to the nature of today's baseball business beast, you can be assured we'll never see his like again.

OPPOSITE: After he left the playing field, Connie Mack always wore a suit to the games, moving players around the field by gesturing with a program or scorecard.

POLL BALLOT

Until fan voting was restored in 1970, managers, coaches, and players voted for the All-Star starters. Here is the ballot filled out by Casey Stengel, then managing the Mets.

INSTRUCTIONS

1. All players, coaches and managers who have at least 30 consecutive days in the league prior to voting are eligible to vote.

2. Each eligible voter is to choose a player for each position listed on reverse side.

3. No voter may choose any player from his own club.

4. Ballots are to be signed as a protection check for the poll, but no individual's ballot will be made public without the voter's approval.

5. Your league's team will be representing you. Make your choices carefully.

FORD FRICK
Commissioner

1964 ALL-STAR POLL BALLOT

POS. *Manager* NAME *Casey Stengel* CLUB *N.Y. Mets*

C	Torre	Milwaukee
1B	White	St. Louis
2B	Mazeroski	Pittsburg.
3B	Santo	Chicago
SS	Groat	St. Louis
LF	Williams	Chicago
CF	Mays	San Francisco
RF	Clemente	Pittsburgh

Casey Stengel
Signature

N.Y. Mets Mgr!
Club

TELEGRAM

Shortly after Casey Stengel was fired as manager of the Brooklyn Dodgers on October 4, 1936, he was honored at a dinner hosted by the New York sportswriters. Commissioner Kenesaw Mountain Landis sent him this telegram on October 8, the day of the dinner.

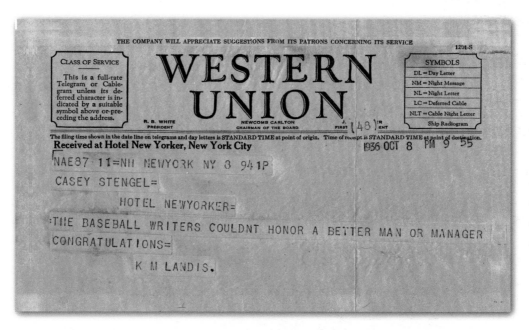

THE COMPANY WILL APPRECIATE SUGGESTIONS FROM ITS PATRONS CONCERNING ITS SERVICE

1201-S

WESTERN UNION

CLASS OF SERVICE

This is a full-rate Telegram or Cablegram unless its deferred character is indicated by a suitable symbol above or preceding the address.

R. B. WHITE
PRESIDENT

NEWCOMB CARLTON
CHAIRMAN OF THE BOARD

J. FIRST 148 'R ENT

SYMBOLS

DL = Day Letter
NM = Night Message
NL = Night Letter
LC = Deferred Cable
NLT = Cable Night Letter
Ship Radiogram

The filing time shown in the date line on telegrams and day letters is STANDARD TIME at point of origin. Time of receipt is STANDARD TIME at point of destination.

Received at Hotel New Yorker, New York City

1936 OCT 8 PM 9 55

NAE87 11=NH NEWYORK NY 8 941P

CASEY STENGEL=

HOTEL NEWYORKER=

THE BASEBALL WRITERS COULDNT HONOR A BETTER MAN OR MANAGER
CONGRATULATIONS=

K M LANDIS.

OPPOSITE: Casey Stengel, keeping close watch on his team.

6

THE
PIONEERS, UMPIRES, AND EXECUTIVES

Baseball is played by the players, but it is run by others on the field and off (with the notable exception of the short-lived 1890 Players' League, of course). The Hall of Fame recognizes these people by inducting umpires who call the game on the field, as well as league and team executives who organize the sport away from the diamond. These are people (among them, the Hall's only female inductee) who have organized the leagues, built the ballparks, signed the contracts, and run "The Show." Though not usually as famous as the wondrous players they worked with, they are nonetheless an integral part of the story of the success of baseball.

Another group of people enjoy a special place in the Hall as Pioneers. As the Hall was born and grew, the founders looked back at the very early days of baseball and sought out those people whose off-field contributions helped to create the foundation for the game we love today. A writer, an early manager, and a person who was part of one of the first amateur baseball clubs are just a few of the people so honored.

Only a few of these men knew the joy of feeling a bat as a solid hit came off it or the thrill of striking out a batter, but the sport they and we love—baseball— would be poorer without their many contributions.

OPPOSITE: John "Jocko" Conlan wasn't afraid to stand up to anyone who chose to argue with him.

ALEXANDER CARTWRIGHT

Though mythmakers tried to claim otherwise, there is no one "father of baseball." Instead, the game grew evolutionarily from a collection of older bat-and-ball games. However, a group of clubs in the New York area in the 1840s were instrumental in beginning to codify and refine these many games into what could be called early baseball. At the heart of the Knickerbocker Base Ball Club was Cartwright, a clerk who loved to play the game. He was secretary of the club that wrote the first set of rules and he was present at the "first match" under those rules. Oddly, the Knickerbockers lost that game, on June 19, 1846, to the New York Nine. Cartwright went West with the Gold Rush a few years later, but his and his club's mark on the game was set.

HENRY CHADWICK

Baseball off the field is a game of words and numbers, and a pioneer of baseball reporting and record keeping was a former cricket-loving Englishman who became a newsman in the greater New York City area. Chadwick saw in baseball something new and fresh and set about becoming its ace chronicler. He is credited with developing the modern box score and also for introducing key statistical records. His writing spread the deeds of the players and the rules of the game for more than 40 years, a time that was essentially formative to the National Pastime.

NESTOR CHYLAK

Among the handful of umpires in the Hall of Fame, Chylak stands out for his universal reputation for fairness. All umps are fair, of course, but others gained their fame for other virtues. Chylak was regarded far and wide as a man all sides could trust. He umpired in the AL from 1954 through 1978 and took part in five World Series.

JOCKO CONLAN

Usually, when a player or manager enters into an argument with an ump, it's mostly one-sided. Not so with 24-year NL ump John "Jocko" Conlan. He famously traded shin kicks with Leo Durocher, who forgot that Conlan had his home plate shin guards under his pants. The one-time boxing referee umped in five World Series, too.

OPPOSITE: Alexander Cartwright went west with the Gold Rush in 1849 and ended up living his later years in Hawaii, where he's pictured here in his role as a fire official.
TOP: Henry Chadwick's enthusiasm for his adopted country and game led to innovations that are still a part of baseball today.
RIGHT: Nestor Chylak

PAT GILLICK

From nothing to the world champion: Pat Gillick built the expansion Toronto Blue Jays into two-time World Series champs, the team he ran from 1977 to 1994. A 27-year general manager, Gillick moved on to helm the Orioles, Mariners, and Phillies. He capped off his legendary career with a 2008 Series title in Philadelphia.

DOUG HARVEY

God. That was Doug Harvey's nickname: God. Seriously, what more do you need to know about an umpire so widely respected that he was deified? He ruled his games for 31 years, serving in the NL and overseeing five World Series. Blessed be the umps.

CAL HUBBARD

Hubbard is, of course, the answer to a famous trivia question: Who is the only person enshrined in both the Baseball and Football Halls of Fame? He got the football nod from a nine-year career as a lineman that included four NFL titles. He earned his baseball accolade from an umpiring career that included 16 well-respected seasons on the field and, following a 1951 eye injury, 18 more as a supervisor of other umps.

*TOP: **Pat Gillick***
*ABOVE: **Doug Harvey***

BAN JOHNSON

Without Bancroft Johnson, the National League might be alone in the world of big league baseball. The former sportswriter had become president of the Western League in 1894. In 1901, he gathered some of that minor league's team owners and other businessmen to form the American League as a rival to the established National League. Through early fits and starts, Johnson's drive kept the AL alive. By 1903, the World Series was born and Johnson began to assert more and more power. For nearly 20 years, Johnson was the uncrowned "czar of baseball."

KENESAW MOUNTAIN LANDIS

In 1920, baseball needed someone to save it from itself. In the wake of the 1919 World Series "Black Sox" scandal and amid constant bickering among owners, players, and others, baseball was becoming unmanageable. The owners decided to impose order on themselves by appointing a commissioner who would rule on all matters relating to the game. They got more than they bargained for in the person of Judge Kenesaw Mountain Landis. The former federal judge ruled with an iron fist for 25 years, banning eight "Black Sox" to start and continuing to kick out any players he felt were not living up to the trust of the game.

TOP LEFT: *Ban Johnson was the first president of the American League.*
TOP RIGHT: *Kenesaw Mountain Landis originated the role of the commissioner.*
RIGHT: *Cal Hubbard.*

EFFA MANLEY

Manley made history in 2006 when she became the first woman elected to the Baseball Hall of Fame. Making history was nothing new to her, however, since she was also the first woman to own a baseball team. She and her husband Abe owned the Eagles of the Negro National League, which played first in Brooklyn and then in Newark. Manley was a force in the front office, working diligently to promote her club and draw fans, while also holding firm against men who tried to push her around. Her 13 years running the Eagles until 1948 saw the Negro Leagues at their height of popularity, in which she played no small part.

LARRY AND LEE MACPHAIL

While the Waners, the Wrights, and the Fosters are the only playing brothers in the Hall (not counting Dan Brouthers, of course), another family pair had a big effect on the game away from the field. Larry MacPhail was a general manager and part-owner of the Reds, Dodgers, and Yankees before and after World War II. A true wheeler-dealer, he saw the future of radio and stadium entertainment and was instrumental in bringing them to the game. His son Lee, a general manager of the Orioles and Yankees, became the AL president and played a key part in player relations negotiations. The ALCS MVP trophy is named for Lee MacPhail.

TOP: *Effa Manley was a groundbreaker in the front office . . . and in the Hall of Fame.*
LEFT: *Larry MacPhail*
ABOVE: *Lee MacPhail*

MARVIN MILLER

Few people have had as big an impact on modern baseball as this determined labor leader. Marvin Miller led the Major League Baseball Players Association through the epic changes from the old reserve system to free agency, setting the stage for today's enormous salaries and player rights. He ran the organization from 1966–1982 and championed the players' cause through work stoppages and a 1981 strike. His legacy is seen every time a star player signs an enormous new contract or a rookie makes more than Mickey Mantle ever did.

HANK O'DAY

O'Day became the tenth umpire inducted into the Hall. He wore the black suit for 30 seasons and was involved in four no-hitters and the famous 1908 Cubs-Giants game in which Fred Merkle didn't touch second base and the NL race had to be decided by a playoff weeks later. O'Day was also a player, manager, and league executive in more than 40 years devoted to pro baseball.

BRANCH RICKEY

Though Rickey is justly celebrated as the visionary executive who signed Jackie Robinson in 1945 and saw him break baseball's "color line" two years later, his influence on baseball is wider still. The former catcher became a lawyer, coach, and executive with four clubs. With the Cardinals in the 1920s, he basically invented the farm system, the organization of minor league teams affiliated with a big-league team. He brought in the first pitching machines and always looked for new and different ways of training players. He moved to Brooklyn in 1942, setting the stage for his great racial coup. He later helped run the Pirates and many of the players he brought carried Pittsburgh to its 1960 World Series. Though reputed to be a harsh negotiator, Rickey's role in creating what baseball is today is undisputed.

TOP LEFT: Branch Rickey
TOP RIGHT: Hank O'Day
ABOVE: Marvin Miller

JACOB RUPPERT

He built Yankee Stadium (the first one). He signed Babe Ruth. The team he owned won seven World Series. Jacob Ruppert's business sense, bold moves, and good luck helped his New York Yankees change the face of baseball. The beer magnate bought the team in 1915 and owned them until his death in 1939.

JOHN SCHUERHOLZ

The players make the plays and the coaches call them, but the general manager is the one who puts the pieces for success in place. John Schuerholz did just that wherever he worked, starting with a 1985 World Series title in Kansas City. He earned even greater rewards in his next stop, Atlanta, where his Braves teams won 14 straight NL East titles, five NL pennants, and the 1995 World Series. That last accomplishment made him the first GM to take home the trophy with a team in each league.

BUD SELIG

Selig cut his baseball teeth owning part of the old Milwaukee Braves in the 1960s. In 1970, he bought the Seattle Pilots and moved them to his hometown, creating the Milwaukee Brewers. He owned the team until 1992, quickly making a mark behind the scenes as a very influential owner. But that year, his fellow owners called on him to become the interim Commissioner of Major League Baseball. He took over the job officially in 1998 and held it until 2015. Under Selig, baseball went through steroid scandals and a strike, but also enjoyed its longest run of financial success and expansion. Revenues throught the game grew to an amazing $9 billion during his impactful time in office.

TOP: Jacob Ruppert
ABOVE LEFT: John Schuerholz
ABOVE RIGHT: Bud Selig

ALBERT SPALDING

Al Spalding started as an ace pitcher but ended up a great baseball businessman. Even while pitching for two pro teams (and leading his league in wins for six straight years, with a high of 54 in 1875), Spalding was setting an empire in motion. When the NL was formed in 1876, he was the manager of the Chicago franchise that won the first pennant. Later that year, he formed a company that soon made all the NL's baseballs. He also published the first of what would be decades of annual guides to the game. By 1882, he was president of the White Stockings, too, and a major force in NL politics. Meanwhile, his sporting goods company grew and remains today a well-known name. From pitcher to powerhouse, few men had as much impact on early baseball as Spalding.

BILL VEECK

That's Veeck as in "wreck," of course, and for most of 35 years, he tried to wreck baseball traditions and bring entertainment and style to the sport. While with the Cubs, he was the man who planted ivy on Wrigley Field's brick walls. As owner of the Indians, he signed Larry Doby as the first African American in the AL and also brought Satchel Paige to the majors, then helped the team set an attendance record and win the 1948 World Series (their last). As the owner of the Browns, he sent little person Eddie Gaedel to the plate (uniform number: ⅛). As owner of the White Sox (twice), he created the exploding scoreboard and put a shower in the bleachers. No one loved having fun at a ballpark more than Veeck, who was baseball's ultimate showman.

GEORGE AND HARRY WRIGHT

We end our tour of the Hall near the beginning of the sport. The "other" Wright brothers were present at the creation of the first all-professional team. Harry Wright was the manager and George Wright the star shortstop of the 1869 Cincinnati Red Stockings, which became the first team to pay its players. They did pretty well, too, winning 81 straight games. George, for his part, played Harry's game to perfection, moving on to play in the National Association and in the new National League in 1876.

TOP LEFT: Always innovative and enthusiastic, Bill Veeck was one baseball's most colorful figures.
ABOVE AND LEFT: Pioneering brothers Harry (top) and George Wright.

STORYTELLERS

You can't go to every game in person, though isn't it lovely to ponder that possibility? However, thanks to the writers who report on the games and the broadcasters who describe them, fans everywhere can and have enjoyed experiencing or reliving baseball's greatest moments.

The Hall of Fame recognizes the importance and contributions of writers and broadcasters with two special annual awards. The J. G. Taylor Spink Award, named for the longtime editor of *The Sporting News*, is given to a writer "for meritorious contributions to baseball writing." The Ford C. Frick Award, named for the postwar commissioner of baseball, is presented annually for major contributions to baseball broadcasting.

Here's a list of the winners of those awards. How many have you heard? How many have you read? And who do you think should be next?

J. G. TAYLOR SPINK AWARD

WRITER	YEAR	WRITER	YEAR	WRITER	YEAR
Nick Cafardo	2020	Joseph Durso	1995	Edgar Munzel	1977
Jayson Stark	2019	Wendell Smith	1993	Harold Kaese	1976
Sheldon Ocker	2018	Leonard Koppett	1992	Red Smith	1976
Claire Smith	2017	Bus Saidt	1992	Tom Meany	1975
Dan Shaughnessy	2016	Ritter Collett	1991	Shirley Povich	1975
Tom Gage	2015	Phil Collier	1990	John Carmichael	1974
Roger Angell	2014	Jerome Holtzman	1989	James Isaminger	1974
Paul Hagen	2013	Bob Hunter	1988	Warren Brown	1973
Bob Elliot	2012	Ray Kelly	1988	John Drebinger	1973
Bill Conlin	2011	Jim Murray	1987	John F. Kieran	1973
Bill Madden	2010	Jack Lang	1986	Dan Daniel	1972
Nick Peters	2009	Earl Lawson	1985	Fred Lieb	1972
Larry Whiteside	2008	Joe McGuff	1984	J. Roy Stockton	1972
Rick Hummel	2006	Ken Smith	1983	Frank Graham	1971
Tracy Ringolsby	2005	Si Burick	1982	Heywood C. Broun	1970
Peter Gammons	2004	Allen Lewis	1981	Sid Mercer	1969
Murray Chass	2003	Bob Addie	1981	Harry G. Salsinger	1968
Hal McCoy	2002	Joe Reichler	1980	Damon Runyon	1967
Joe Falls	2001	Milton Richman	1980	Grantland Rice	1966
Ross Newhan	2000	Bob Broeg	1979	Charles Dryden	1965
Hal Lebovitz	1999	Tommy Holmes	1979	Hugh Fullerton	1964
Bob Stevens	1998	Tim Murnane	1978	Ring Lardner	1963
Sam Lacy	1997	Dick Young	1978	J. G. Taylor Spink	1962
Charley Feeney	1996	Gordon Cobbledick	1977		

(Note: The Spink Award was not given in 1994; the gap listed in 2007 is due to a change in when the award winner was named and presented.)

ABOVE: Cubs and Cardinals fans heard Harry Caray's voice for decades. He also worked for Oakland and the White Sox.

THE FORD C. FRICK AWARD

BROADCASTER	YEAR	BROADCASTER	YEAR	BROADCASTER	YEAR
Ken Harrelson	2020	Jerry Coleman	2005	By Saam	1990
Al Helfer	2019	Lon Simmons	2004	Harry Caray	1989
Bob Costas	2018	Bob Uecker	2003	Lindsey Nelson	1988
Bill King	2017	Harry Kalas	2002	Jack Buck	1987
Graham McNamee	2016	Felo Ramirez	2001	Bob Prince	1986
Dick Enberg	2015	Marty Brennaman	2000	Buck Canel	1985
Eric Nadel	2014	Arch McDonald	1999	Curt Gowdy	1984
Tom Cheek	2013	Jaime Jarrin	1998	Jack Brickhouse	1983
Tim McCarver	2012	Jimmy Dudley	1997	Vin Scully	1982
Dave Van Horne	2011	Herb Carneal	1996	Ernie Harwell	1981
Jon Miller	2010	Bob Wolff	1995	Russ Hodges	1980
Tony Kubek	2009	Bob Murphy	1994	Bob Elson	1979
Dave Niehaus	2008	Chuck Thompson	1993	Mel Allen	1978
Denny Matthews	2007	Milo Hamilton	1992	Red Barber	1978
Gene Elston	2006	Joe Garagiola	1991		

THE COMPLETE LIST

The following is a complete list of **The National Baseball Hall of Fame** members:

A

Aaron, Henry L. "Hank" 1982
Alexander, Grover C. 1938
Alomar, Roberto 2011
Alston, Walter E. 1983
Anderson, Sparky 2000
Anson, Adrian C. "Cap" 1939
Aparicio, Luis E. 1984
Appling, Lucius B. "Luke" 1964
Ashburn, Don R. "Richie" 1995
Averill, H. Earl 1975

B

Bagwell, Jeffrey R. 2017
Baines, Harold D. 2019
Baker, J. Franklin 1955
Bancroft, David J. 1971
Banks, Ernest 1977
Barlick, Albert J. 1989
Barrow, Edward G. 1953
Beckley, Jacob P. 1971
Bell, James T. "Cool Papa" 1974
Bench, Johnny L. 1989
Bender, Charles A. "Chief" 1953
Berra, Lawrence P. "Yogi" 1972
Biggio, Craig A. 2015
Blyleven, Bert 2011
Boggs, Wade 2005
Bottomley, James L. 1974
Boudreau, Louis 1970
Bresnahan, Roger P. 1945
Brett, George H. 1999
Brock, Louis C. 1985
Brouthers, Dennis "Dan" 1945
Brown, Mordecai P. 1949
Brown, Raymond 2006
Brown, Willard 2006
Bulkeley, Morgan G. 1937
Bunning, James P. D. 1996
Burkett, Jesse C. 1946

C

Campanella, Roy 1969
Carew, Rodney C. 1991
Carey, Max G. 1961
Carlton, Steven N. 1994
Carter, Gary E. 2003
Cartwright Jr., Alexander J. 1938

Cepeda, Orlando M. 1999
Chadwick, Henry 1938
Chance, Frank L. 1946
Chandler, Albert B. "Happy" 1982
Charleston, Oscar M. 1976
Chesbro, John D. 1946
Chylak Jr., Nestor 1999
Clarke, Frederick C. 1945
Clarkson, John G. 1963
Clemente, Roberto W. 1973
Cobb, Tyrus R. 1936
Cochrane, Gordon S. 1947
Collins, Edward T. 1939
Collins, James J. 1945
Combs, Earle B. 1970
Comiskey, Charles A. 1939
Conlan, John B. "Jocko" 1974
Connolly, Thomas H. 1953
Connor, Roger 1976
Cooper, Andy 2006
Coveleski, Stanley A. 1969
Cox, Robert J. 2014
Crawford, Samuel E. 1957
Cronin, Joseph E. 1956
Cummings, William A. 1939
Cuyler, Hazen S. "Kiki" 1968

D

Dandridge, Raymond E. 1987
Davis, George S. 1998
Dawson, Andre N. 2010
Day, Leon 1995
Dean, Jay H. "Dizzy" 1953
Delahanty, Edward J. 1945
Dickey, William M. 1954
Dihigo, Martin 1977
DiMaggio, Joseph P. 1955
Doby, Lawrence E. 1998
Doerr, Robert P. 1986
Dreyfuss, Bernhard "Barney" 2008
Drysdale, Donald S. 1984
Duffy, Hugh 1945
Durocher, Leo E. 1994

E

Eckersley, Dennis 2004
Evans, William G. 1973
Evers, John J. 1946

Ewing, William B. "Buck" 1939

F

Faber, Urban C. "Red" 1964
Feller, Robert W. A. 1962
Ferrell, Richard B. 1984
Fingers, Roland G. 1992
Fisk, Carlton 2000
Flick, Elmer H. 1963
Ford, Edward C. "Whitey" 1974
Foster, Andrew "Rube" 1981
Foster, Willie H. 1996
Fox, Nelson J. 1997
Foxx, James E. 1951
Frick, Ford C. 1970
Frisch, Frank F. 1947

G

Galvin, James F. "Pud" 1965
Gehrig, H. Louis 1939
Gehringer, Charles L. 1949
Gibson, Joshua 1972
Gibson, Robert 1981
Giles, Warren C. 1979
Gillick, Pat 2011
Glavine, Thomas M. 2014
Gomez, Vernon L. "Lefty" 1972
Gordon, Joseph L. 2009
Goslin, Leon A. "Goose" 1968
Gossage, Richard "Goose" 2008
Grant, Frank 2006
Greenberg, Henry B. 1956
Griffey Jr., George K. 2016
Griffith, Clark C. 1946
Grimes, Burleigh A. 1964
Grove, Robert M. "Lefty" 1947
Guerrero, Vladimir 2018
Gwynn, Anthony K. "Tony" 2007

H

Hafey, Charles J. "Chick" 1971
Haines, Jesse J. "Pop" 1970
Halladay, Harry Leroy 2019
Hamilton, William R. 1961
Hanlon, Edward H. "Ned" 1996
Harridge, William 1972
Harris, Stanley R. "Bucky" 1975
Hartnett, Charles L. "Gabby" 1955

Harvey, Harold Douglas "Doug" 2010
Heilmann, Harry E. 1952
Henderson, Rickey N. H. 2009
Herman, William J. 1975
Herzog, Dorrel "Whitey" 2010
Hill, Pete 2006
Hoffman, Trevor W. 2018
Hooper, Harry B. 1971
Hornsby, Rogers 1942
Hoyt, Waite C. 1969
Hubbard, R. Cal 1976
Hubbell, Carl O. 1947
Huggins, Miller J. 1964
Hulbert, William A. 1995
Hunter, James A. "Catfish" 1987

I

Irvin, Monford "Monte" 1973

J

Jackson, Reginald M. 1993
Jackson, Travis C. 1982
Jenkins, Ferguson A. 1991
Jennings, Hugh A. 1945
Jeter, Derek S. 2020
Johnson, Byron B. "Ban" 1937
Johnson, Randall D. 2015
Johnson, Walter P. 1936
Johnson, William J. "Judy" 1975
Jones, Larry W. "Chipper" 2018
Joss, Adrian 1978

K

Kaline, Albert W. "Al" 1980
Keefe, Timothy J. 1964
Keeler, William H. "Willie" 1939
Kell, George C. 1983
Kelley, Joseph J. 1971
Kelly, George L. 1973
Kelly, Michael J. "King" 1945
Killebrew, Harmon C. 1984
Kiner, Ralph M. 1975
Klein, Charles H. 1980
Klem, William L. 1953
Koufax, Sanford 1972
Kuhn, Bowie K. 2008

★ ★ ★

L

La Russa, Anthony 2014
Lajoie, Napoleon "Larry" 1937
Landis, Kenesaw M. 1944
Larkin, Barry L. 2012
Lasorda, Thomas C. 1997
Lazzeri, Anthony M. 1991
Lemon, Robert G. 1976
Leonard, Walter F. "Buck" 1972
Lindstrom, Frederick C. 1976
Lloyd, John H. 1977
Lombardi, Ernest 1986
Lopez, Alfonso R. 1977
Lyons, Theodore A. 1955

M

Mack, Connie 1937
Mackey, Biz 2006
MacPhail, Leland S. "Larry" 1978
MacPhail Jr., Leland S. 1998
Maddux, Gregory A. 2014
Manley, Effa 2006
Mantle, Mickey C. 1974
Manush, Henry E. "Heinie" 1964
Maranville, Walter J. "Rabbit" 1954
Marichal, Juan A. 1983
Marquard, Richard W. "Rube" 1971
Martinez, Edgar 2019
Martinez, Pedro J. 2015
Mathews, Edwin L. 1978
Mathewson, Christopher 1936
Mays, Willie H. 1979
Mazeroski, William S. 2001
McCarthy, Joseph V. 1957
McCarthy, Thomas F. 1946
McCovey, Willie L. "Stretch" 1986
McGinnity, Joseph J. 1946
McGowan, William A. 1992
McGraw, John J. 1937
McKechnie, William B. 1962
McPhee, Bid 2000
Medwick, Joseph M. 1968
Méndez, José 2006
Miller, Marvin J. 2020
Mize, John R. 1981
Molitor, Paul 2004
Morgan, Joe L. 1990
Morris, Jack 2018

Murray, Eddie C. 2003
Musial, Stanley F. 1969
Mussina, Michael C. 2019

N

Newhouser, Harold 1992
Nichols, Charles A. "Kid" 1949
Niekro, Philip H. 1997

O

O'Day, Henry M. 2013
O'Malley, Walter F. 2008
O'Rourke, James H. 1945
Ott, Melvin T. 1951

P

Paige, Leroy R. "Satchel" 1971
Palmer, James A. 1990
Pennock, Herbert J. 1948
Pérez, Tony 2000
Perry, Gaylord 1991
Piazza, Michael J. 2016
Plank, Edward S. 1946
Pompez, Alex 2006
Posey, Cumberland Willis Jr. 2006
Puckett, Kirby 2001

R

Radbourn, Charles G. 1939
Raines, Timothy 2017
Reese, Harold H. "Pee Wee" 1984
Rice, Edgar C. "Sam" 1963
Rice, James E. "Jim" 2009
Rickey, W. Branch 1967
Ripken Jr., Calvin E. "Cal" 2007
Rivera, Mariano 2019
Rixey, Eppa 1963
Rizzuto, Philip F. 1994
Roberts, Robin E. 1976
Robinson Jr., Brooks C. 1983
Robinson, Frank 1982
Robinson, Jack R. 1962
Robinson, Wilbert 1945
Rodríguez, Iván 2017
Rogan, Wilber J. 1998
Roush, Edd J. 1962
Ruffing, Charles H. "Red" 1967
Ruppert Jr., Jacob 2013

Rusie, Amos W. 1977
Ruth, George H. "Babe" 1936
Ryan, Lynn Nolan 1999

S

Sandberg, Ryne 2005
Santo, Ronald E. 2012
Santop, Louis 2006
Schalk, Raymond W. 1955
Schmidt, Michael J. 1995
Schoendienst, Albert F. 1989
Schuerholz, John 2017
Seaver, George T. 1992
Selee, Frank G. 1999
Selig, Allan H. "Bud" 2017
Sewell, Joseph W. 1977
Simmons, Aloysius H. 1953
Simmons, Ted L. 2020
Sisler, George H. 1939
Slaughter, Enos B. 1985
Smith, Hilton 2001
Smith, Lee A. 2019
Smith, Ozzie 2002
Smoltz, John A. 2015
Snider, Edwin D. "Duke" 1980
Southworth, William H. "Billy" 2008
Spahn, Warren E. 1973
Spalding, Albert G. 1939
Speaker, Tristram E. 1937
Stargell, Wilver D. "Willie" 1988
Stearnes, Turkey 2000
Stengel, Charles D. "Casey" 1966
Sutter, Howard Bruce 2006
Suttles, Mule 2006
Sutton, Donald H. 1998

T

Taylor, Ben 2006
Terry, William H. 1954
Thomas, Frank E. 2014
Thome, James H. 2018
Thompson, Samuel L. 1974
Tinker, Joseph B. 1946
Torre, Joseph P. 2014
Torriente, Cristóbal 2006
Trammell, Alan 2018
Traynor, Harold J. "Pie" 1948

V

Vance, Arthur C. "Dazzy" 1955
Vaughan, Joseph F. "Arky" 1985
Veeck, Bill 1991

W

Waddell, George E. "Rube" 1946
Wagner, John P. "Honus" 1936
Walker, Larry K. 2020
Wallace, Roderick J. 1953
Walsh, Edward A. 1946
Waner, Lloyd J. 1967
Waner, Paul G. 1952
Ward, John M. 1964
Weaver, Earl S. 1996
Weiss, George M. 1971
Welch, Michael F. 1973
Wells Sr., Willie 1997
Wheat, Zachariah D. 1959
White, James L. "Deacon" 2013
White, Sol 2006
Wilhelm, James Hoyt 1985
Wilkinson, J. Leslie "J. L." 2006
Williams, Billy L. 1987
Williams, Joe "Smokey Joe" 1999
Williams, Richard H. "Dick" 2008
Williams, Theodore S. 1966
Willis, Victor, G. 1995
Wilson, Jud 2006
Wilson, Lewis R. "Hack" 1979
Winfield, David M. 2001
Wright, George 1937
Wright, William H. "Harry" 1953
Wynn, Early 1972

Y

Yastrzemski, Carl M. "Yaz" 1989
Yawkey, Thomas A. 1980
Young, Denton T. "Cy" 1937
Youngs, Ross M. 1972
Yount, Robin R. 1999

ABOUT THE AUTHOR

James Buckley Jr. has written more than 150 books on sports for readers young and old, including biographies of sports heroes Roberto Clemente, Lou Gehrig, Babe Ruth, Jesse Owens, and Muhammad Ali. He has also written and produced a dozen annual editions of the *Scholastic Year in Sports*. Among his baseball titles are *Obsessed with Baseball*, *Classic Ballparks*, *Perfect: The Story of Baseball's 23 Perfect Games*, and *Eyewitness Baseball*. He has also written about football, basketball, soccer, and other sports, and worked for *Sports Illustrated* and NFL Publishing. Since 2000, he has run the Shoreline Publishing Group, a California company that produces sports and other books for national publishers. When he's not writing, he has spent 25 years as one of the organizers (and occasional radio and PA voice) of the seven-time national-champion Santa Barbara Foresters, a summer college baseball team. Buckley's first visit to the Hall of Fame was in 1989, when he attended the induction ceremony of Carl Yastrzemski, his boyhood hero. He has returned to the Hall with his family. . . and expects to go back again and again.

*BELOW, LEFT TO RIGHT: **Christy Mathewson, Carl Yastrzemski, and Ken Griffey Jr.***

IMAGE CREDITS

Every effort has been made to trace copyright holders. If any unintended omissions have been made, Epic Ink would be pleased to add appropriate acknowledgments in future editions.

All images are courtesy of the National Baseball Hall of Fame and Museum, Cooperstown, New York, unless otherwise noted below.

Cover: Shutterstock

Page 12: (top) Glasshouse Images / Alamy Stock Photo, (bottom) History and Art Collection / Alamy Stock Photo

Page 16: (right) National Baseball Hall of Fame and Museum / Charles Conlon

Page 17: (top) National Baseball Hall of Fame and Museum / Charles Conlon

Page 18: National Baseball Hall of Fame and Museum / Charles Conlon

Page 19: (bottom) Mark Rucker/Transcendental Graphics, Getty Images

Page 20: National Baseball Hall of Fame and Museum / Charles Conlon

Page 29: (left) National Baseball Hall of Fame and Museum / Doug McWilliams

Page 34: (images 1, 2, 3, and 5, from top) ©iStockphoto.com/spectruminfo; (image 4) ©iStockphoto.com/justinkendra

Page 37: (bottom) Sporting News Archive / Contributor / Getty Images

Page 39: (bottom) Eugene Buchko / Shutterstock

Page 41: National Baseball Hall of Fame and Museum / Doug McWilliams

Page 43: Rich Pilling / Stringer / Getty Images

Page 45: (top) National Baseball Hall of Fame and Museum / Rich Pilling

Page 44: (bottom) Chris Trotman / Stringer / Getty Images

Page 47: Jim McIsaac / Contributor / Getty Images

Page 48: Anthony Correia / Shutterstock

Page 49: National Baseball Hall of Fame / Milo Stewart Jr.

Page 50: National Baseball Hall of Fame and Museum / Doug McWilliams

Page 52: (left) National Baseball Hall of Fame and Museum / Rich Pilling, (right) Jeff Gross / Staff / Getty Images

Page 53: National Baseball Hall of Fame and Museum /Rich Pilling

Page 64: (bottom) Kidwiler Collection/Diamond Images/Getty Images

Page 68: (top left) National Baseball Hall of Fame and Museum / Rich Pilling, (top right) Focus On Sport / Contributor / Getty Images, (bottom left) Paul Buck / Contributor / Getty Images

Page 75: (bottom left) Stephen Dunn / Staff / Getty Images

Page 77: © Bettmann/CORBIS

Page 80: National Baseball Hall of Fame and Museum / Doug McWilliams

Page 81: SPX/Diamond Images / Contributor / Getty Images

Page 82: (top) Bettmann / Contributor / Getty Images

Page 83: (right) Tony Tomsic / Contributor / Getty Images

Page 84: Focus On Sport / Contributor / Getty Images

Page 85: Focus On Sport / Contributor / Getty Images

Page 92: Rick Stewart / Stringer / Contributor / Getty Images

Page 93: (top) Focus On Sport / Contributor / Getty Images, (bottom) SPX/Diamond Images / Contributor / Getty Images

Page 96: (left) National Baseball Hall of Fame and Museum / Charles Conlon

Page 98: Bettmann / Contributor / Getty Images

Page 103: (right) Ron Vesely / Contributor / Getty Images

Page 104: (right) Photo Works / Shutterstock

Page 107: (top) Bettmann / Contributor / Getty Images

Page 109: George Gojkovich / Contributor / Getty Images

Page 112: (bottom) Diamond Images / Getty Images

Page 113: Brace Hemmelgarn / Contributor / Getty Images

Page 115: (top right) Ron Vesely / Contributor / Getty Images

Page 121: Focus On Sport / Contributor / Getty Images

Page 125: National Baseball Hall of Fame and Museum / Charles Conlon

Page 132: (top) Otto Greule Jr / Stringer / Getty Images

Page 134: (right) Mark Rucker / Transcendental Graphics / Getty Images

Page 141: (top) National Baseball Hall of Fame and Museum / Charles Conlon, (bottom left and center) National Baseball Hall of Fame and Museum / Chickering

Page 150: (top) Focus On Sport / Contributor / Getty Images

Page 151: (left) Baltimore Sun / Contributor / Getty Images

Page 152: (top) Tony Tomsic / Contributor / Getty Images

Page 155: (left) Brian Bahr / Staff / Getty Images

Page 156: SPX/Diamond Images / Contributor / Getty Images

Page 157: (left) Ron Vesely / Contributor / Getty Images, (right) Joe Robbins / Contributor / Getty Images

Page 159: Focus On Sport / Contributor / Getty Images

Page 167: (right) National Baseball Hall of Fame / Charles Conlon

Page 169: (top) Focus On Sport / Contributor / Getty Images

Page 170: (bottom left) Focus On Sport / Contributor / Getty Images

Page 171: Vincent Laforet / Staff / Getty Images

Page 180: Jeff Goode / Contributor / Getty Images

Page 182: Mark Rucker/Transcendental Graphics / Getty Images

Page 183: (bottom) National Baseball Hall of Fame and Museum / Milo Stewart Jr.

Page 190: (left) National Baseball Hall of Fame and Museum / Charles Conlon, (middle and right) National Baseball Hall of Fame and Museum / Doug McWilliams